LAUGH YOUR TROUBLES AWAY

The Complete History of Riverview Park

CHICAGO, ILLINOIS

by Derek Gee and Ralph Lopez

1st Edition

Manufactured in the United States of America.

ISBN 0-9676045-1-6

Sharpshooters Productions, Inc. offers a companion video tape. For
information call or write: 734.762.6621, Sharpshooters Productions,
Inc., 17902 Myron, Livonia, MI 48152-3121.

To the People of Chicago:

Who loved Riverview for 63 years.

ACKNOWLEDGMENTS

Bringing the splendor of Riverview Park back to the public has been a labor of love for us. The authors wish to gratefully acknowledge the following people and institutions, without whose generous contributions of time, personal stories, photographs and films, and historic documents, this book would not have been possible.

Jim Abbate

Diane Abbate

Mike Anderson

Norman D. Anderson

Stan Barker

Mike Batson

Mike Chew

The Chicago Historical Society

Eugene Feerer

Ann M. Gee

Patricia Gee

Charles J. Jacques, Jr.

Rich Juvinall

Tom Keefe

Howard Lange

Library of Congress

Gary Mack

Noel Mattai

National Archives

The National Amusement Park Historical Association (NAPHA)

The Ravenswood-Lakeview Historical Society

The Carousel News and Trader

Matt Spinello

Walter Schaeffer

Derek Gee and *Ralph Lopez*
December 1999

My first experience at Riverview came about perched atop my father's shoulders going through the front Western Avenue gate over forty-five years ago. It is my distinct pleasure to contribute this foreword to a fabulous book about a place we thought would never close. Riverview is as much about Chicago's history as the Water Tower or Michigan Avenue.

To generations of Chicagoans it was a place to "Laugh Your Troubles Away." Nearly two million people visited the park that final season until it was officially over on October 3, 1967. *Laugh Your Troubles Away - The Complete History of Riverview Park* is a clear and concise work on one of Chicago's, if not the nation's, most beloved amusement parks.

This glorious book, in my opinion, will stand the test of time as the definitive reference volume on Riverview Park. Riverview Park was more than just summer fun; it was a part of Chicago tradition, an embodiment of six decades and an ever-changing reflection of those times.

What Derek Gee and Ralph Lopez have accomplished is nothing less than a chronicle of not only Riverview's history, but the all around good feeling one might experience having visited there. Riverview Park was present through four wars and the Great Depression. This park preceded radio and television as one of the public's main sources of summer entertainment.

This book, well researched over several years, captures this history and brings the park to life in its words and pictures. Throughout this work, the reader is truly brought back in time to experience this amusement park up close and personal. Decade by decade, the reader will see the way changes in the park that took place were representative of the times.

On a personal note, it has been my extreme pleasure to have been associated first as host and associate producer on *Laugh Your Troubles Away - The Complete History of Riverview Park*, the companion video, as well as this book. In my opinion, they both complement each other.

So turn on the lamp, sit back in that easy chair, and prepare to take a journey back in time when all of us could "Laugh Our Troubles Away" at a magical place once known as Riverview Park.

Norm Cherry
December 1999

Norm Cherry: Born and raised in Chicago, Norm is a TV Producer/Director and an Emmy Award Nominee. Norm has his Master's degree in Mass Communications from Southern Illinois University at Carbondale.

CONTENTS

CHAPTER ONE

BEFORE RIVERVIEW

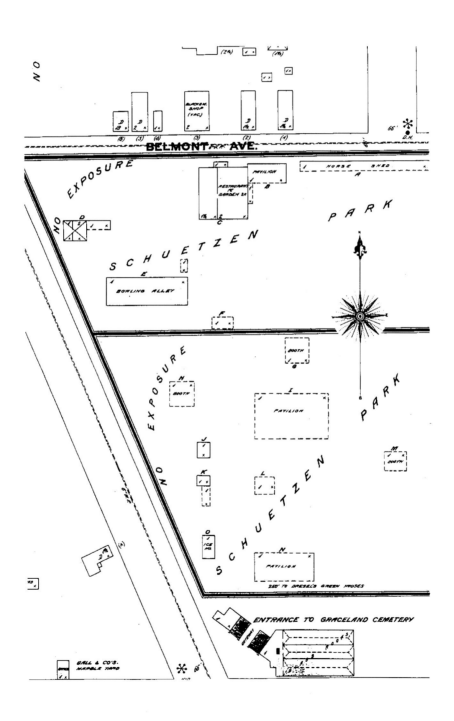

This Carousel was built by the E. Joy Morris Company for Sharpshooters Park, prior to its name change to Riverview. Located near the front gate, it remained in operation through the 1912 season. Courtesy of the Chicago Historical Society ICHi29365.

To anyone who lived in Chicago, chances are that fond memories remain of a place called Riverview Park. It was a special place where families could enjoy a picnic, ride a carousel or roller coaster, or just stop to watch the fun.

Riverview's history begins at the corner of Western Avenue and Roscoe Street in the year 1879. This area of Chicago was settled largely by German immigrants, many of whom were veterans of the Prussian War. The Kriegs Varein, roughly meaning War Club, was a national group for German War veterans. The Chicago chapter was incorporated in 1876. To keep their marksmanship up to date, a

number of the Kriegs Varein formed a separate group called "Der Nord Chicago Schuetzenverein", which translated to the North Chicago Shooters Club. This club purchased acreage from George Bickerdike and his wife on August 25, 1879. In February of 1888, "Der Nord Chicago Schuetzenverein" sold this land to the newly formed "North Chicago Sharpshooters Association."

These "Sharpshooters" cleared away a portion of their 22 acre plot of land to use as a shooting range. Reportedly, hanging targets were strung from the trees on a small island in the the Chicago River, which at that time, cut through the the property. The rest of the wooded land was used for picnics by the members and their families. The park was dubbed "Schuetzen Park" by the Germans and "Sharpshooters Park" by the the locals, who eventually began asking the private club if their grounds could be rented for special occasions.

Legend has it that while at the "Sharpshooters" outings the wives and children of the men grew bored after lunch when the men attended to their target practice. To ease the complaints, the members decided to purchase a carousel. Whether this carousel was human, animal, or steam powered, and exactly what year this

Kriegs Verein Group.

A pleasant walk in Riverview around 1906.

happened is undetermined, but the story was told by the Schmidt family many times and follows the trend of what was happening elsewhere in Chicago and the world.

At the Chicago World's Columbian Exposition of 1893, a separate area called the Midway Plaisance was set aside for amusements. The Midway Plaisance was such a success that soon parks all over the country began adding rides to attract customers. In 1894, Sharpshooters Park contained only restaurants, beer booths, and a bowling alley, but by 1896, when the park hosted Presidential candidate William Jennings Bryan, a carousel, Ferris Wheel, and even games of chance had been added to the eastern side of the park. It should be noted that while people were perched atop the music stands and beer booths to get a glimpse of Mr. Bryan, sizable numbers of people had absolutely no interest in the speech and remained at the amusements.

William Jennings Bryan addressing the Labor Day meeting at Sharpshooters Park.

CHAPTER TWO
RIVERVIEW IS BORN

Just inside the park entrance, 1906.

William M. Johnson

George Schmidt

Wilhelm Schmidt

George Goldman

Around the turn of the century, the Sharpshooters Association dissolved and two members purchased the land from the club. They were Wilhelm (William) F. Schmidt, a prosperous baker located at 81 Clybourne Avenue, and his partner George Goldman. Schmidt may have been thinking about "going commercial" with the park for some time because he had purchased land from the club as early as September of 1892. However, for reasons unknown, he sold it back to the club in December, 1893. A State Bank Trust purchased this land on March 25, 1901. The "North Chicago Sharpshooters Association" is supposed to have disbanded around this time, although the Chicago Kreigs Verein continued into the late 1920's. Schmidt and Goldman operated the park as a picnic ground until 1903, when Schmidt's son, George, returned from Europe. George was sent to Germany for his high schooling, and during his travels, he visited large amusement parks like Copenhagen's Tivoli Gardens and the Prater in Austria. George Schmidt suggested to his father that they make Sharpshooters Park more like the European parks.

For the 1903 season, Schmidt and Goldman opened the park to the general public, who previously had to rent the entire grounds in a group in order to use it. A manager named J. W. Bush was hired to handle the expanded picnic business. In early 1904, a Pittsburgh area banker, Joseph R. McQuaide, and William M. Johnson, a Chicago area lawyer, leased the grounds from Schmidt and Goldman. It is unclear why this "Eastern syndicate", as it was referred to in one local paper, was brought in to turn the small picnic ground into the "World's Largest Amusement Park." Perhaps the Schmidts could not raise the necessary capital themselves or were simply unwilling to assume the risk. Johnson and McQuaide renamed the park "Riverview" and advertised it as "Riverview Sharpshooters Park" to retain name recognition. It is possible, although not certain, that McQuaide suggested the name Riverview after visiting a popular Riverview Park on the north side of Pittsburgh. The Pittsburgh Riverview contained an astronomical observatory and later, a carousel, and was in full swing during the late 1890's, so it seems plausible that it was McQuaide who brought the name to Chicago.

Johnson and McQuaide provided financing for new attractions, such as a midway, a figure-8 shaped roller coaster called The White Flyer, Shooting the Rapids (a combination of a slow water ride with a small Shoot-the-Chutes), The Temple of Mirth (a funhouse with a mirror maze and distortion mirrors), A Trip to the Mines, and a Helter Skelter slide. On opening day, July 2, 1904, there was no admission fee, and crowds packed the park. Other featured attractions were the Hiawatha Village where "Sioux" Indians fought U.S. Troops, a balloon race between Professor Morrison of Montreal, Canada and a Miss DeVonda of Chicago, and the Radium Palace, which featured light effects.

The 1st Imperial Marine Band of Germany provided the music that day. The local Musicians Union chapter almost stopped the performance by filing a grievance against them with the national organization. They were angry that the members of this German band were not members of their union. Luckily for Riverview, the Musicians Union Grievance Committee denied their claims and the 1st Imperial Marine Band went on as scheduled. Transportation to the park was easy, since the city's trolley cars already ran up Clybourne Avenue to the park, and a steamboat named "Welcome" took people from the Clark Street bridge downtown to the park via the Chicago River. It should be noted that the evening of July fourth brought the first accident at Riverview, when a 22-year-old man named Jacob Bolk fell out of the White Flyer and broke his leg.

Oddly enough, while Johnson and McQuaide signed their partnership agreement granting them part of the Riverview property in April of 1904, Schmidt didn't sign the agreement until AFTER the season was over in September, 1904! Perhaps if Riverview had failed, the deal would have been called off. Even stranger, McQuaide gave his land located in the middle of the Riverview site to George Schmidt, in return for some land George owned that was closer to Western Avenue. At this point McQuaide disappears from the Riverview story, never to be heard from again. However, the park was so successful that in 1905, the partnership was dissolved and the Riverview Sharpshooters Park Corporation was formed.

The White Flyer - a figure 8 style roller coaster.

CHAPTER THREE

EXPANSION!

Marine Causeway, Riverview Exposition, Chicago, Ill.

Marine Causeway

In 1906, the park expanded to 50 acres in size and added $500,000 worth of new attractions including: Over the Waves, Rollin's Wild Animal Arena, a Dancing Pavilion (later used as a Roller Rink in the '40's), an Igorrote Indian Village from the Philippines, an Ostrich Farm, and a Crocodile Ranch. Also added was an attraction that was the forerunner of today's virtual reality rides called Hale's Tours of the World. Riders boarded railroad cars to be transported to exotic places around the world. This was simulated by rocking the railroad cars and projecting films of the destinations into the windows as patrons peered out.

The Igorrote Indian Village arrived at Riverview in 1906.

A peculiar ride called the Double Whirl began operating in the latter part of 1906. Built in Chicago by the Double Whirl Manufacturing Company, six Ferris Wheels revolved around a central post, giving a different kind of thrill.

The Double Whirl was an interesting variation on the Ferris Wheel.

Laugh Your Troubles Away

Riverview's Second Dancing Pavillion, built in 1906, was later used as a roller skating rink.

Riverview's first Dancing Pavilion sat among picnic groves. A completely covered Dancing Pavilion was later built along Belmont Ave.

Expansion!

The most famous ride added that year was the Aero-Stat, later renamed the Strat-O-Stat. Built by a local firm, the Federal Construction Company, the ride consisted of six cars that were suspended from a central mast. As the ride rotated and reached its top speed of 30 miles an hour, passengers felt the sensation of flight. Initially, it was located at the front of the park and later relocated beside the Shoot-The-Chutes around 1908. Sometime during the mid-teen's, biplane-shaped cars replaced the original ones. By the 1930's, the biplanes were replaced with cars shaped like rocket ships and the ride was renamed Strat-O-Stat.

The Aero-Stat, seen in its original location near the front gate in 1906.

Riverview claimed to have the smallest train in the world in 1906.

The Fall of the Pompeii fireworks was the big evening spectacle. A new Casino building housed an elaborate restaurant with flowers, trees, and a fountain. Sometime before 1910, probably in 1907, the Casino expanded by placing the entire structure up on jacks, and constructing a new first floor.

The Casino Building after its third floor was added.

The Casino Building, prior to the addition of a third floor.

Expansion!

Nicholas P. Valerius

In 1907, the growing park attracted more investors. The previous Riverview Sharpshooters Park Corporation dissolved, and a new Riverview Park Company took its place. The new officers, Paul W. Cooper, and Nicholas P. Valerius, brought much additional capital to the firm. That year, the $550,000 spent on the park added 40 more acres, constructed the area of the park known as the "Pike", named after the 1904 World's Fair amusement midway, and laid the grounds out for years to come. As the season opened, advertisements trumpeted "All other parks beaten to a frazzle!"

Paul W. Cooper

The famous front gate photographed about 1920.

Laugh Your Troubles Away

New for 1907 was a magnificent front gate with handsome lattice-work and electric lights. In the 1920's, the lattice-work was covered over, but the gate remained beautiful until the park's end in 1967. A lagoon was dug and equipped with row boats and motor boats for men to rent to take their young ladies out in. Also added was an automobile race track, the $50,000 Velvet Coaster, and the Hellgate and Top rides. William H. Strickler of the Federal Construction Company designed the Velvet Coaster. It was a silky smooth coaster with very small dips - hence the "Velvet" part of the name. It was claimed that the coaster cost $50,000 and was 4700 feet long. The Top was one of the most unusual roller coasters ever built, in that it was shaped like a top, and as the trains went around it, it wobbled like a top. The Top was operated by a concessionaire who apparently left the park at the end of July 1916 season. A Top ride, perhaps the same one, later appeared at Luna Park, Coney Island, at the beginning of the 1917 season.

Riverview's Top Coaster premiered in 1907.

Expansion!

This view of the newly constructed Velvet Coaster gives a better look at the sign.

The Velvet Coaster was known for its velvety smooth ride.

Hellgate was a boatride that began with a circular whirlpool, which was supposedly the entrance to Hell, and then took riders past scenes of Satan's domain. On July 31, 1909, John S. Reid, Jr. wrote his friend Hilda Sweet a detailed letter describing a trip to Riverview. He describes the entrance to Hellgate as "The apparatus of a spiral-shaped trough filled with water through which the boats travel at a little slower pace than a walk. Upon reaching the center of the spiral, the speed of the boats increases and shooting down an incline they disappear from view. At several points on the route passengers are confronted by these signs of warning [Keep Hands Inside of Boats]."

Riverview's Hellgate ride, was a simulated trip to Hades.

The view of the Marine Causeway from across the river, 1908.

Expansion!

The Pikes Peak Scenic Railway entrance, circa 1908.

To provide another roller coaster for the 1907 season, Riverview turned to the builder of its first coaster and the Shooting the Rapids ride, the Ingersoll Engineering and Construction Company of Pittsburgh. An up-and-coming Homewood, Illinois, native named John A. Miller engineered the Pikes Peak Scenic Railway for Ingersoll, and its construction would begin a long relationship between Miller and Riverview. Miller, often described as the Thomas Edison of roller coasters because of his numerous important patents, would go on to become the premier American roller coaster designer.

A new park area called Fairyland, named after a section of the 1904 St. Louis Fair amusement area, was constructed and one of Riverview's

most memorable rides placed in it — the Shoot-The-Chutes. Built at a cost of $50,000, riders experienced the thrills of a dark ride, while sailing in the entrance tunnel, and a water ride, with a soaking splashdown controlled by a boatman who rode along. Riverview patron Norm Cherry recalls, "In addition to getting a little wet when you hit the pond going down, some boatmen would intentionally rock the boat in the back and cause the girls to panic!" For its opening, the ride sported a huge monster face surrounding the entrance tunnel, and a sign at the top of the tower that read, "Shoot the Chutes in Fairyland." The sign was nearly identical to the one that adorned the Shoot the Chutes at the 1904 World's Fair.

The first season for the Shoot-the-Chutes, 1907. Notice that the Aero-Stat and Carousel building have not been built yet.

Laugh Your Troubles Away

The owner of the Shoot-The-Chutes was Charles R. Francis, who had previously owned the "Chutes" at Chutes Park located at Kedzie and Jackson Streets, just west of downtown Chicago. When Chutes Park closed at the end of 1906, Francis needed a new place to do business, so he was granted the concession at Riverview and built a new, enlarged Chutes ride. Francis' own firm, the Federal Construction Company, designed the ride and several other rides for the park.

The Marine Causeway, or River Walk was started in 1907 and later completed with the construction of the Monitor and Merrimac attraction in 1908.

A new Marine Causeway, also known as the River Walk, was built in 1907 along the Chicago River at the rear of the park and a baseball diamond was constructed off Addison Avenue. Allegedly owned by Chicago White Sox owner Charles Comiskey, patrons could watch semi-professional baseball games on Saturday and Sunday. Another novelty, Roller Skating, was presented in the new rink, located inside the picnic groves at the back of the park. A new park ride, the Aquarasel, was a water merry-go-round, and allegedly the first in the nation. Among the interesting promotions that year was a Baby Contest where the top prize was a $500 piano. The 100 second prizes were bank books with one dollar in it to start baby's savings, along with five dollars worth of baby photos.

By 1908, Riverview expanded to 102 acres and was now the most popular park in Chicago. This success allowed Riverview to secure the best attractions. An impressive new John Miller designed roller coaster, named the Royal Gorge Scenic Railway, took riders up fifty-two feet on the first hill. The park claimed that it cost $150,000 to build, although that figure is probably an exaggeration. An unusual suspended coaster called the Aerial Coaster or later the Pottsdam Railway, was built by another local company, the Aerial Tramway Construction Company. The cars were suspended below the track instead of riding on top of it. While suspended coasters are commonplace today, at the turn of the century, they were new and rare.

The Pottsdam Railway and the Monitor & Merrimac are shown here about 1908.

Expansion!

The short-lived Aerial Coaster, shown here around 1909, after its name change to Pottsdam Railway, only lasted three seasons before being removed for the first Blue Streak roller coaster. Courtesy of the Chicago Historical Society ICHi-22574.

The Royal Gorge Scenic Railway entrance.

"On the Dip at Riverview Park". This photo is the Royal Gorge Scenic Railway.

Expansion!

The Pikes Peak Scenic Railway loading platform. Note the elaborate scenery surrounding the ride.

The most incredible new attraction for 1908 was a $240,000 re-creation of the Civil War battle between the Monitor and Merrimac, which was housed in an elaborate building located along the Marine Causeway. The show used paintings, models, sound effects, and smoke to recreate the historic battle. Interestingly, the Walt Disney Company proposed building a Monitor and Merrimac attraction for their aborted Virginia history theme park, Disney's America, in 1994.

Close-up view of the Monitor & Merrimac show, 1908.

Another popular ride added that year was the Thousand Islands, probably named for the resort islands in New York where millionaires played. Later park-goers would know it as Mill on the Floss, taking the title of George Eliot's 1860 novel, Tunnel of Love, or the Old Mill. This ride was another designed by the Federal Construction Company. Says Norm Cherry, "I remember this was a great Friday and Saturday night date ride. Young teens would try to stop the boats by grabbing onto the grass adjacent to the waterways. This would panic the young lovers in the back of the boats!"

The Thousand Islands ride was completely surrounded by the Velvet Coaster.

The Thousand Islands ride was Riverview's second water ride, replacing in 1908 an earlier ride located near the main gate.

Expansion!

Looking west inside the Thousand Islands ride.

A postcard view of the front of the Thousand Islands ride, 1908.

Laugh Your Troubles Away

Riverview's famous carousel was also installed this year in the Fairyland section. In January of 1908, park concessionaire Fidelity Amusement Company contracted with the Philadelphia Toboggan Company (PTC) to build one of the largest carousels ever constructed, with five rows of horses. The ornate building that it was placed in was built by the Keystone Amusement Company. The carousel was designated by the manufacturer as PTC #17, and it contained 70 hand-carved horses and two eleven-foot chariots decorated with embracing lovers and a surprised looking Cupid. Plaster Cupids, birds, donkeys, rabbits, and trees decorated the outer rim. Included with the carousel were two Band Organs supplied by the firm, Gaviloi and Company. One organ, a 65 key Gavioli model, used cardboard punched with holes to store the music, and the other, a 65 key Waldkirch Company product, presumedly used punched paper rolls to store the music.

Shipped from Philadelphia by rail, Charles Bowditch accompanied the carousel to take charge of the set-up. Gustav Weiss and Leo Zoller, PTC's master painter and master carver, also came along to handle any touch-ups the machine or horses might require. PTC intended to take great care erecting one of the most ornate carousels ever built!

Riverview's fabulous Carousel was one of the largest ever built, holding five rows of large horses.

Expansion!

Riverview's original E. Joy-Morris built new carousel was located just inside the main gate and continued to operate through the 1912 season!

To pay for this stupendous carousel, Fidelity Amusement put a chattel mortgage on Riverview's Velvet Coaster, which it also owned. Total cost for the carousel, to be paid in four installments, was $18,000, plus transportation charges and the set-up experts' expenses. PTC #17 had many famous riders over the years including Tom Mix, Clara Bow, President Warren G. Harding, William Randolph Hearst, and Al Capone. Norm Cherry remembers, "What a fast merry-go-round! You wouldn't dare try to jump off. Those hand-carved horses seem large even as an adult!" It should be noted that even with the addition of PTC #17, the E. Joy Morris built carousel at the front of the park still continued to operate through the end of the 1912 season.

Also constructed was a 215 foot observation tower called the Eye-full Tower. The park made many exaggerated claims of its size, at one point claiming it was 275 feet. However, according to surviving blueprints and insurance maps, it was in fact, 215 feet from the base to the tip of its iron structure. With the addition of the ten-feet flagpole, it brought it up to the 225 feet number mentioned in various newspapers. The tower was glass walled, with lights on the sides and had pneumatic tube elevators to visitors up to the top. Unfortunately, the Chicago building authorities condemned the structure two weeks after it opened because they deemed the air-pressure elevators to be unsafe. The original builder of the Eye-full, the Iron Observation Tower Company, appears to have gone bank-

Riverview's majestic Carousel, circa 1908.

The Carousel building with the Aerial Coaster (aka Pottsdam Railway) at left.

Expansion!

Repainting the animals on the Carousel was done regularly at Riverview.

A close-up view of the Shoot-the-Chutes elevator.

The Eye-Full tower with the Derby sign at right.

rupt as the result of the closing, and it was later sold to another company. The tower sat unused until 1916, when reportedly equipped with a more conventional elevator, it finally opened to the public. In 1936, it was converted into a parachute drop.

Other attractions for 1908 included an outdoor show called The Fight of the Little Big Horn which advertised 350 Indians, soldiers, and mustang horses. Late in the season, on August 29th, a ride called the Whirlpool opened after repeated delays. It seems unusual that a new ride would be opening so late in the year since the park closed shortly after Labor Day. The Whirlpool designed by Ingersoll Engineering, consisted of freewheeling cars that were brought to the center of a rotating disk. As the disk got up to speed, the cars flew outward in a dizzy manner. A short-lived park mascot simply called "The Little Lady of Riverview" debuted at the beginning of the 1908 season. The "Little Lady" mascot was only used twice early in the season, and must have been ineffective as it was never used again.

"The Little Lady of Riverview"

Expansion!

These men just might be Riverview's semi-pro baseball team. This postcard was sold along with two cards of the House of David amusement park team. Located in Benton Harbor, Michigan, they would have been nearby opponents for the Riverview team.

Baseball was played at Riverview starting in 1907. The baseball field was in the middle of the automobile racing track at the rear of the park. Note the Riverview smock on the dog at the bottom center of the photo. Also note the large billboard for Edelweiss beer.

Laugh Your Troubles Away

Tours of the World

View along Pike.

Looking East on the Pike, 1907.

Expansion!

A view looking along the Pike section of the park shows a few interesting attractions such as the Rag Time Jubilee Singers, the Electric Theatre, and a movie theatre showing The Kansas Cyclone.

Riverview's claim to be the most popular park in Chicago is borne out by this crowded scene near the front gate. Photo taken during the 1906 season.

Laugh Your Troubles Away

Near the Entrance stands from left to right, Aqua and her Water Nymphs, the House of Laughter, the 3rd. Degree, and a Helter Skelter slide.

The games booth along the Pike, 1906

A Gypsy fortune teller, circa 1907

CHAPTER FOUR

RIVERVIEW EXPOSITION PARK

Concert Garden, Riverview Park around 1907.

The magnificent Creation Building.

Another landmark year for the park was 1909. According to park publicity material, the name changed to Riverview Exposition Park in order to "better convey an adequate idea of the extent of its marvels." The success of the 1893, 1901, and 1904 World's Fairs obviously inspired the park's managers to cash in on the craze. Changing the name would help to differentiate Riverview from its competitors. Why go to an ordinary "park" when one can go to an "Exposition"? The topography of Riverview was also changed that year as the Chicago River, which curved deeply through the property, was straightened from Belmont to Addison Avenues. Park management hoped that patrons would arrive by boat from Evanston and Wilmette, Illinois, but it is unknown if this ever happened.

The Creation show, a copy of the attraction at the 1904 World's Fair and Coney Island, cost $320,000 to construct, and was placed in a magnificent, 210 feet long building with a Lagoon in front. The show simulated the Biblical version of the Earth's creation, using 85 feet high moving scenery, live organ and choir performances of Hayden's Oratorio, and appropriate sound effects. Inside the theater, the audience sat in wicker chairs and peered through portholes while the scenery moved by on belts.

Other rides added that year included the Tickler, the Witching Waves, and the Expo Whirl. The Witching Waves was a popular ride in many parks around the country. Riders rode steel "waves" in a open-front car around an oval track. Many attendants had to be placed around the ride to give the cars a push when they got stuck within a wave. The Tickler featured a circular car that spun and bumped down a slanted facade, much like the steel ball in a pinball machine. It seems more like an ouch than a tickle! The Expo Whirl was a renamed Merry Widow Whirl made by an unknown ride manufacturer. The ride consisted of two Ferris wheels mounted side by side, supported by a common axle. The wheels had no need for additional outside support structures because of its clever design. The park shows that year included Buffalo Bill's Wild West and Pawnee Bill's Far East combined shows, an amateur talent contest called Duncan Clark's Hook Bazar [sic] where 35 people "got the hook" every fifteen minutes. The same year, a new theater designed for Paul W. Cooper was screening a motion picture titled Seven Temptations of Good Old St. Anthony. Will de Wegstaffe, a columnist for the New York Times, thought Riverview was so incredible he wrote, "Riverview Exposition in Chicago has more shows and rides then the combined offerings of Luna Park, Dreamland, and Steeplechase Parks at gay Coney Island, and the people enjoy them samely." Chicagoans sure did! For just the 1909 season, opening day attendance was 157,863 and for the entire year, seven million had visited Riverview!

The Witching Waves ride was new and popular during the 1909 season. Courtesy of Chicago Historical Society ICHi-29364.

Laugh Your Troubles Away

A song, specially written for the park, was popular and Riverview published the lyrics, but not its title, in a newspaper ad. The lyrics were:

I'll see you tonight
Out at Riverview, Riverview, Riverview!
And sorrow will vanish for me
And for you out at Riverview!
We'll coast on the Coaster
And roller skate, roller skate,
Take in all the shows and
We'll dance until late
Out at Riverview!

Later, in 1911, a waltz entitled "Let's All Take a Trip Out to Riverview" was written by Glenn W. Ashley, with words by Paul A. Sellke and Edward M. Brooks. Sellke and Brooks just happened to be the song's Chicago-based Publishers. The lyrics are:

If you're feeling lonesome, don't know where to go,
There's a place on the north side of town,
A place of amusement for young and old
'Tis the best that ever was found.

It's the park they call Riverview, park of all parks,
And everything right up to date, Shooting the Chutes,
Looping the Loop, And riding the figure eight.

Chorus

Let's all take a trip out to Riverview,
And have one jolly good time;
Be one of the boys or one of the girls,
And you'll always be right in line.

There's dancing, skating, sports of all kinds,
There's music afloat in the air,
And there isn't a park of all other parks
That with Riverview can compare.

You may talk of New York or of old Rockaway,
You may talk about Coney Isle,
There's a place in Chicago, it's dear Riverview,
That has them all beaten a mile.

Every evening and on Sunday, too,
We all go out for a lark,
Dressed in our best, we take our girl
For a trip out to Riverview Park!

Repeat Chorus

A beautiful lady on the Man in the Moon, circa 1907. The message on the back of the card is by a photographer who indicates what type of film, lighting and exposure he used for the shot. The photographer mentions that this photo came out better than the other photographer he was comparing himself to.

Posing with an "exotic" automobile was popular in Riverview's photo studio around 1909.

Looking down the lift hill of the Derby racing coaster during its construction, 1910. Note the White Flyer Figure 8 coaster is at right, and the Royal Gorge Scenic Railway at upper left. The Pikes Peak Scenic Railway is at middle left. Courtesy of the Chicago Historical Society ICHi-29363.

More thrills came in 1910 with the addition of The Derby racing coaster, where two trains raced side by side. Constructed by the Ingersoll Engineering and Constructing Company for park concessionaire P. J. Schaefer, once again, it was designed by John Miller. While the structure looks enormous in photographs due to its width, The

Derby's lift hill was only 66 feet tall. The rest of the ride was a series of gentle, undulating, double-dip drops and lateral turns. The Derby was one of Ingersoll's Racer Dips models and other similar racing coasters by Ingersoll/Miller popped up all over the country usually under the name Derby Racer.

This side view of the Derby Racing Coaster gives a better idea of its size.

The Derby Racing Coaster was the hit of the 1910 season.

The Atlantic Beach was the other main addition for the 1910 season. A 400 x 175 foot swimming pool, it was surrounded with white sand. The wading end of the pool went to four and a half feet deep, while at the other end, where the 70 feet high diving tower was located, the depth went to fourteen feet. Private lockers accomodated 1500 people, and Riverview claimed that it was the world's largest, artificial, swimming pool. The construction took longer than expected and bad weather during the following two seasons took its toll and the pool was filled-in by 1913.

On May 18th, 1911, the park hosted a "Halley's Comet" party, cashing in on the curiosity and fear surrounding the famous comet's arrival. Many people believed that the comet heralded doom, and others thought that the poisonous cyanogen gas in the tail of the comet would kill them, it seems brave that Riverview adopted a "Let's Party!" atmosphere. The park's profits soared that evening as people gathered to watch Halley streak through the night sky!

The short-lived Atlantic Beach swimming pool lasted only two seasons!

Riverview Exposition Park

Riverview's Midway, circa 1910.

Always trying to drum up business, the park made a $5,000 offer for the first Teddy Roosevelt speech made in the park before September 18th. Roosevelt was on a summer speaking tour trying to unify the Republican Party and was drawing huge crowds wherever he went. It is not known if the Schmidt's were Republicans or whether they just remembered the size of the crowds that William Jennings Bryan brought to the park in 1896.

Other $5,000 offers were made for the winner of the Jefferson-Johnson fight, if made before July 15th, and the start of the New York - Chicago Airship Race, but apparently no one followed up on their offers. Additional park features for 1910 included a model dairy farm with eight milking cows and 100 chickens, and a mummy from the sealed caves of Cliff Dwellers, probably a native American from the Southwest. The park also added 38 acres of land to bring the total size to 140 acres.

The Band Shell where John Phillip Sousa and Arthur Pryor's Band played.

Laugh Your Troubles Away

Panoramic View from the Chutes.

Look at the long lines on this summer's day!

The Carousel, Aero-Stat, and Shoot-the-Chutes at night.

Riverview Exposition Park

Football at Riverview, played next to the Derby coaster during the 1910 season.

The Frolic Ride, circa 1909.

Laugh Your Troubles Away

Boats entering the Shoot-the-Chutes tunnel at right.   Note the goat track at left.

Shoot the Chutes - Night scene.

A Shoot-the-Chutes boat splashing down right in front of the Velvet Coaster.

The Miniature Railway on the Marine Causeway, 1914.

Riverview's police force, circa 1909.

Laugh Your Troubles Away

The River Walk at night was a beautiful sight to see!

Riverview's Main Gate at night, circa 1909.

Riverview Exposition Park

Refreshment Corner, somewhere in Riverview about 1906.

The Games Booth along the Pike, 1906.

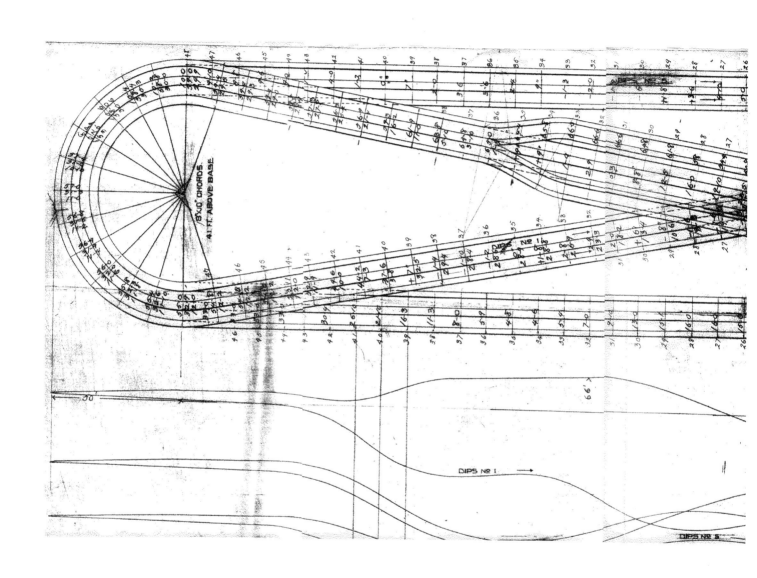

DIPS Nº 1 →

DIPS Nº 5

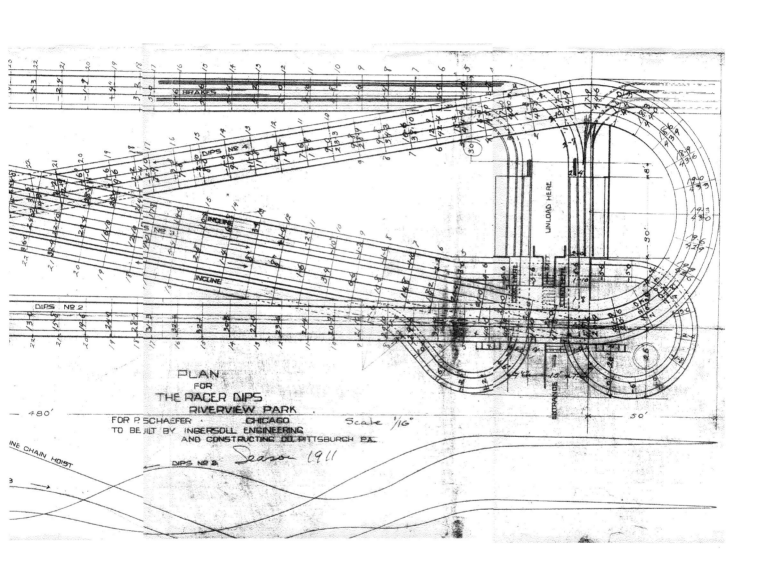

PLAN
FOR
THE RACER DIPS
RIVERVIEW PARK
FOR P. SCHAEFER · CHICAGO   Scale 1/16"
TO BE BILT BY INGERSOLL ENGINEERING
AND CONSTRUCTING CO. PITTSBURGH P.A.
Season 1911

The Derby Racer Blueprint

CHAPTER FIVE
THIEVES IN THE PARK

The Carousel building, about 1911. Note the original gondola shaped cars on the Aero-Stat at left.

The original Blue Streak roller coaster, built in 1911.

A nice overview of the 1911 Blue Streak coaster. Note the covered tunnels at right.

The Aerial Coaster (a.k.a. Pottsdam Railway) was removed for 1911 and another roller coaster, the first Blue Streak, took its place. It was one of designer John Miller's Speed-O-Plane model coasters, and was located next to, and wrapped around the Monitor and Merrimac building. The Blue Streak surely benefitted from its proximity to that popular attraction.

Laugh Your Troubles Away

The other side of the Blue Streak roller coaster, 1911.

The original Blue Streak coaster was built around the Monitor and Merrimac building in 1911.

A close-up of the Blue Streak track. The side friction boards that helped keep it on the track are clearly visible on either side.

Riverview also became the first amusement park to open a Motordrome for motorcycle racing that year. Located at the north end of the picnic grounds and constructed at a cost of $40,000, it provided seating for 30,000 people. The track was one-third of a mile in length and banked at a 45-degree angle. Each motorcycle race consisted of three laps around the track to make up one mile. The racers belonged to the Motorcycle League, which paid for transportation to and from the park. A cash purse of $500 was given by the League to the driver with the highest number of points at the end of the season. Indian brand motorcycles were used exclusively. The cycles had eight valve engines which were speed adjusted to one-fifth of a second variation, so that the rider's skill would be the only variable in the race. Spectators could sit inside the center paddock for a quarter or in the grandstand for fifty and seventy-five cents.

The park also constructed a smaller, 70 foot long Autodrome for racing autos. Owned by Henry J. Cohn, two 2200 pound Staver racing autos zoomed at 60 miles an hour on the saucer shaped track. The track was banked at 78 degrees and was up to 18 feet high, 22 feet if measured from the ground rather than the base of the track. The races consisted of thirty-two laps or one mile in length.

On August 13th, in a blatant attempt to horn in on the International Aviation Meet in Grant Park, Riverview offered $250 in gold to the first aviator to land in the Motordrome between 4:30pm and 5:00pm. It is unknown whether any aviator detoured and landed in the park, but the park made no mention of the feat in subsequent ads.

The Motorcyclist posed in the Motordrome with his Indian motorcycle. The photographer's handwritten caption reads "Mike and Wolters."

Riverview's motorcycling racing track, the Motordrome, was built in 1911.

Thieves In The Park

In November of 1911, the park's minority stockholders, led by the Schmidt family, filed suit against the majority stockholders. The minority members listed in the lawsuit were: William Schmidt, who owned 205 shares of stock; George Goldman, 50 shares; George Schmidt, 50 shares, and Augusta Miller with 30 shares. The majority stockholders were: Paul Cooper, with 220 shares of stock; Nicholas Valerius, 247 shares, and William Johnson, who owned 174 shares of stock.

The minority stockholders charged that company officers Cooper, Valerius, and Johnson had cut secret deals with several concessionaires, enriching themselves at the expense of the park. Specifically, the suit charged that Riverview had received an offer from the Monitor and the Merrimac concession to pay the park twenty-five or forty percent of the gross as rent. The three officers refused the offer and counter-proposed to Riverview's Board of Directors that the rent should be ten percent of the gross. Unknown to the rest of Riverview's Board, Cooper, Valerius, and Johnson secretly proposed a deal to the Monitor and the Merrimac managers that would give them one-half of the net concession profits after payment to the park. The concession's managers rejected this and instead proposed to pay Riverview ten percent of the gross and give Riverview one-half interest in the assets and profits of the Monitor and the Merrimac. The suit alleged that the three officers converted this one-half interest to their own use thereby "cheating and defrauding the Riverview Park Company." Similar schemes were used with the operators of the Creation show and the miniature railways. The suit stated that the last four years' profits from the Monitor and the Merrimac totaled $150,000, two years of Creation's profits were $80,000, and the miniature railways made $25,000. Allegedly, half of these amounts were given to the three officers.

In April 1912, the court ruled for the minority, and the Schmidt family became the park managers. William Schmidt served as President, while his son, George Schmidt, was named Secretary. George Goldman became Vice-President. Of the three accused officers, Valerius and Johnson were forced out of the company and their stock was sold to Roland Whitman and William F. Merle. Merle, the principal of Chicago's White City Amusement Park, became the company's new Treasurer. The stock sale to Mr. Merle eventually caused problems in the 1940's and ultimately lead to the park's demise fifty-six years later. Paul Cooper was removed as President, but he remained on the board as a director along with the newly appointed director, Roland Whitman. It may seem peculiar that Cooper was allowed to remain on the board after being sued in a breach of trust case, but unfortunately the reasons for his retention have been lost to the mists of time. As a result of the suit, the Monitor and the Merrimac show appears to have been closed for the 1912 season while a replacement attraction was located.

For Riverview Park, 1912 was a key year. With the Schmidts now in control, many changes were made. The first was the rehiring of Col. James Hulton as Press Agent. Hulton handled the publicity for Riverview's opening season, but later left for more important positions. An article in Billboard stated Hulton was "devising novel stunts to bring in patrons as before." This probably included the park's August hosting of the Chicago Motorcycle Club. Every motorcycle club within a 100 mile radius converged on Riverview for a day's fun.

Laugh Your Troubles Away

The Rarity attraction with the entrance to the Picnic Grounds at right. The Rarity apparently showed films of the Swiss Alps around 1911.

The Creation building became Dante's Inferno, which showed an Italian multi-reel motion picture depicting the Netherworld. Red lights, steam at the entrance, a pipe organ, and a live ladies orchestra added to the illusion of Satan's domain. Other new attractions like the Gee Whiz roller coaster, later known as the Greyhound, were installed to try to bring back the crowds. The coaster was 3500 feet long, and the park trumpeted in advertisements that it was over a mile long. The Gee Whiz (a.k.a. Greyhound), designed by John Miller for Ingersoll Engineering, did not have anything to actually hold the coaster cars to the track.

Photos of the Greyhound or any of the coasters built before it, show vertical boards on either side of the track. The cars had side wheels which rubbed against these guide boards to help keep them on the track. When John Miller invented

the safety under wheels that locked the cars to the track in late 1912, these side boards became unnecessary. Norm Cherry says of the Greyhound, "Everybody started out their coaster riding on this mild coaster, but it was also the longest ride in the park from a time standpoint. You really got your money's worth".

A man named "Daredevil" Schreyer was hired to thrill the crowds with his bicycle/high diver act. As Billboard described, "In this act, Schreyer, after climbing to the top of the starting tower -which is 80 feet high - mounts an ordinary bicycle and whirls at a pace of 100 miles an hour down the steep incline, at the end of which, dropping the machine, he turns a triple somersault in his flight of 185 feet, carooning [sic] gracefully into a pool of water, 7x15 feet, amid the plaudits of the big crowds drawn by this act."

In addition to the new rides and attractions, major improvements were made to the park's grounds. The bandshell was repainted to give it a "soft, calm appearance," and the Casino Restaurant was refurbished.

The Greyhound pictured only a few years after its construction as the Gee Whiz in 1911.

CHAPTER SIX

GOODBYE RIVERVIEW EXPOSITION, HELLO RIVERVIEW PARK!

Aerial photo of park, taken from the Eye-Full Tower about 1914.   Also visible in the photo are a freak show (bottom left), the Gee Whiz coaster (bottom right), the Blue Streak coaster wrapped around Sinking of the Titanic building (top left), the Carousel (top center), Shoot-the-Chutes (top center), the Aero-stat (top center), the Velvet Coaster (top right), and the Casino building (top right).

GOODBYE RIVERVIEW EXPOSITION, HELLO RIVERVIEW PARK!

In 1913, management decided to drop "Exposition" from the Riverview name. The Monitor and the Merrimac show was replaced by a new Sinking of the Titanic show that was a dramatization of the Titanic disaster complete with a Titanic survivor, Albert Horswill, lecturing in the foyer prior to the show. An excited newsboy described the Titanic show to a Billboard reporter in his Chicago tough-guy accent: "A tall guy [Andre Langdon] springs a buncho highbrow stuff, de curt'n goes up. Yer see de boat - den it starts, and after while it hits de iceburg. Wow! and den it sinks (de boat not de berg). Den anudder boat comes breezin' in. I tink

de guy called it de Garfish [the Carpathia] or sumpin' like dat. Anyhow, it's a boat, all right, and den you wait a while and you see Coney Island and Noo Yoik and den Prill, he says, 'This way out' and you beat it". Another man told the same reporter, "Why it's so real, you don't dare eat peanuts, for fear you'll get 'mal de mer' [sea sickness]."

As if the last few month's legal problems weren't enough, rumors circulated in the industry that the majority of the amusement parks in Chicago were unable to pay their debts. While it was true that the cold and rainy weather early that year had reduced business, the parks were a long way from bankruptcy. Luckily, attractions like the Sinking of the Titanic, the Gee Whiz coaster, the daredevil show, and Arthur Pryor's Band continued to do big business.

The only new ride for 1913 was the Gyroplane which appeared late in the season. From the only known picture of the Gyroplane, it seems to be a spinning ride with three arms. Tilted wheels on the end of the arms rotate also, much like a Huss Troika ride today. Dante's Inferno became the Palais Pictorial, which was a "Hippodrome" type movie theater. The most important highlight that occurred in 1913 was the introduction of Riverview's famous Mardi Gras Parade. The Mardi Gras celebration started on the second Saturday before Labor Day, and ran through Labor Day, the last operating day of the park. A large parade of costumed people made their way around the park each night.

The Sinking of the Titanic was new for the 1913 season. Note the sign for the Blue Streak at left.

These Marti Gras floats on this and the following pages are very typical of the type seen at Riverview in the mid-teens - Circa 1914.

Goodbye Riverview Exposition, Hello Riverview Park

A Parade at Marti Gras time!

Laugh Your Troubles Away

One of the many shows presented at the Bandshell, circa 1918.

In the early days, the general public was invited to come in costume and prizes were given for the best ones. The Bandshell Stage was used for the contests. Later, Riverview hired performers to dress up and entertain the crowd. Jugglers, Ice Skaters, Elephants, Clowns, and Hand-Walkers were all part of the parade which usually showcased about 35 floats. In later years, the parade began next to the Water Bug and circled around the park, returning by the Rotor ride. It was a tradition that lasted until the park closed in 1967.

Also held during Mardi Gras was the Tournament of Music. Four Marching Bands from different high schools competed every night for a week. On Labor Day, the seven winning bands performed for the crowd. A Pittsburgh, Pennsylvania Park, Kennywood, picked up Riverview's tradition of a Mardi Gras parade after contacting the Schmidts and traveling to Chicago to view the 1949 Mardi

Gras parade. Kennywood retitled their festivity the Fall Fantasy Parade and it remains a Kennywood tradition to this day.

While the previous two years had been bad, 1914 profits did not turn out much better. Business was down for parks all over the country. The only new ride installed at Riverview was another racing roller coaster, the Jack Rabbit. Designed by the prodigious John Miller, the ride was again built by the Ingersoll Engineering and Construction Company. The Jack Rabbit was advertised in local papers using such slogans as "Get the habit, ride the rabbit." It proved popular with the crowd and was featured on park postcards around that time. The Palais Pictorial turned into War of the Worlds, which was not based on the H.G. Wells novel. Instead, it was a fictional naval battle where the U.S. fleet was attacked by other major world powers. Naturally, the U.S. fleet won.

Goodbye Riverview Exposition, Hello Riverview Park

Looking down a dip on the Jack Rabbit. The mid-course operator booth at center top was where an operator was stationed to watch for trouble and apply brakes if necessary.

Inside the Jack Rabbit trackage.

The brake run on the Jack Rabbit coaster. Some speed kid!

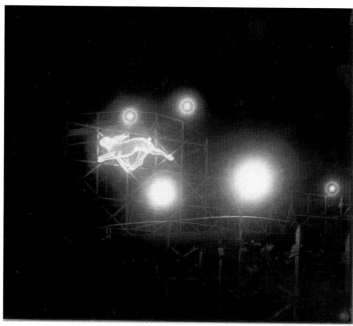

The Jack Rabbit at night.

Goodbye Riverview Exposition, Hello Riverview Park

The entrance to the Jack Rabbit, 1914. The Witching Waves, Gyroplane, and the Derby coaster are also visible.

Other changes for 1914 included replacing the park's midway with new concrete walks, and renaming the Palace Gardens area Palais de Danse.

Paving the Marine Causeway, circa 1914.

Laugh Your Troubles Away

Paving the midway across from the Velvet Coaster, 1914.

The Harpoon, lists champion cyclists from countries such as Australia, Denmark, France, and Italy. A huge grandstand and clubhouse, surrounded the track. The clubhouse was stocked with cycling, athletic, and amusement magazines, as well as the daily papers, for the patrons to read while waiting for the races. Races began at 8 P.M. on Wednesdays, Saturdays, and holidays. The top prizes for the 50 mile amateur team race were four bicycles, two sets of tires, and a few five and ten dollar merchandise orders (gift certificates).

The year 1915 saw the construction of a bicycle racing stadium called the Velodrome, just northwest of the front gate. The name was derived from the bicycle's original name - velocipede. It had a 540 foot long, six-lane track made of cedar wood, which was more resistant to splintering in case of accidents. Racers arrived from all over the globe to compete at Riverview. A surviving 1915 issue of Riverview's weekly cycling magazine,

The War of the Worlds became the Waterdrome, where aquatic shows entertained the crowds. Another new attraction was the Panama Canal, which was a stage show based on the newly constructed canal. In retrospect, the concept of a stage show based on the Panama Canal sounds quite humorous, but was probably quite exotic for 1915.

Paving midway near Jack Rabbit, 1914.

Goodbye Riverview Exposition, Hello Riverview Park

The start of a big bicycle race in the Velodrome, circa 1915.

Riverview's grandstand overlooking the automobile racing track.

Some of the stars riding at the Riverview Velodrome, 1915.

Motorcyclists in the Race for Life attraction.

The freak show performer known as "Lobster Boy."

The Freak show, seen here about 1914, was a Riverview staple until the end of the park.

The War of the Worlds

CHAPTER SEVEN
THE WAR YEARS

Protesting the amusements tax enacted during World War I, circa 1919.

For 1916, Sinking of the Titanic became Battles of a Nation. As World War I raged in Europe, Riverview decided to show German newsreels depicting the war from the "other side." Since Riverview was located in a German neighborhood, the recent immigrants were desperate for news of the war from home. To bring titles such as Battles of a Nation or With the Fighting Germans, and Fighting With Germany (Deutchwehr) to the U.S., the film distributors had to run the British naval blockade of Germany. These films played at the park through the 1916 season and were discontinued when the United States entered the war in April, 1917. With the U.S. on the Allied side now, it would have been unpatriotic to continue to show the German films.

At this same time and for the same reason, an eight-foot statue of Germany's Prime Minister, Otto Von Bismarck, was removed from its site, appropriately called Bismarck Gardens.

In the 1950's, the area surrounding Bismarck Gardens became the miniature golf grounds. Park legend has it that the statue was buried on park grounds. A group of employees tried to find it in the 1960s, but was unable to locate it. Other new attractions for 1916 were the Ostrich and Alligator Farm, a display of Sea Cows (Manatees), and Snoozer, the talking Dog.

This statue of German Statesman Otto Von Bismarck, was removed in 1917 when the U.S. entered on the Allied side in World War I.

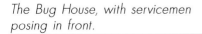

The Bug House, with servicemen posing in front.

Laugh Your Troubles Away

In 1917, the Waterdrome was converted into the Bug House, an elaborate fun house. Built at a cost of $125,000 dollars, it was 50,000 square feet in size. The name Bug House was contemporary slang meaning "nut house" or "crazy house". The front of the building was decorated with large statues of clowns running and doing handstands, along with a few mosquito-like bugs. Large, fanciful bug statues covered the top of the facade. Advertisements proclaimed it as "A million laughs a minute" and "it's the big laugh!"

One of the giant slides in the Bug House. Note the sign for the Human Roulette Wheel at right.

Man feeding ducks in front of Bug House, circa 1919. Note sheep grazing at right.

The War Years

The front of The Bug House.

The Bug House crew, 1917.

Laugh Your Troubles Away

Also added was a Whip ride, which remained popular right up to the end of the park. The Whip, made by the W.F Mangels company, consisted of a series of cars attached to arms that rotate around an oval track. As each car reached the end of the oval, it skittered around the end in a whip-like motion.

Having a good time on the Whip.

The Whip, in its original location at the front of the park, in 1917. The top of the Pippin coaster entrance can be seen above the trees at right.

The Whip before opening time. Note that you can see the top of Big Dipper entrance above left.

Lining up to ride the Whip.

For 1918, Riverview added Over the Falls, which was a higher, steeper Old Mill type water ride with a bigger splash at the end. Over the Falls was designed by the Humphrey Company, owners of Cleveland's Euclid Beach Park, as an improvement in the standard PTC Old Mill ride. Since the Schmidt family were friends with the Humphreys, it was only natural that they shared relevant information.

For 1918, Riverview added Over the Falls, which was a higher, steeper Old Mill type water ride with a bigger splash at the end.

Over the Waves ride, pictured about 1918.

In 1919, three more rides appeared. The Ginger Snap, later known as the Virginia Reel or the Crazy Ribbon, the Winner, which was a Prior & Church racing carousel, and the Cannon Ball roller coaster. Ginger Snap riders boarded a circular tub which was hauled up a slight incline and then released. As it traversed the ribbon-like track on a downhill slope, the cars spun wildly. The Winner was a carousel, but with a difference. The horses not only went up and down, but a special mechanism allowed each set of four horses along the track to move front and back, allowing them to "race". The winner of each race won a free ride.

Riding the Ginger Snap (aka Crazy Ribbon) ride.

The Winner, a Prior & Church Racing Carousel, was at the park from 1919 through the 1925 season.

The Cannon Ball was designed by John Miller of the Miller & Baker Company and Benjamin E. Winslow, Riverview's own engineer, for ride operator Fred Pearce. Originally proposed by Miller for the site of Riverview's existing Royal Gorge coaster, it was actually erected on a small piece of land parallel to Western Avenue at Belmont. The coaster only remained at the park for seven years because concessionaire Pearce's lease expired and the park declined to renew. Riverview wanted the land expand the Western Avenue parking lot as more autos were now coming to Riverview.

The Ginger Snap ride, with the Derby coaster directly behind it, circa 1924.

The big park show that year was the League of Notions, a comic opera spoofing the much serious League of Nations, Woodrow Wilson's failed attempt at a United Nations type body. Riverview's concession manager, Walter Johnson, would meet his future wife Evelyn while she was dancing in League of Notions, and they would marry in March of 1920. It was an event which made the pages of Billboard, the industry newspaper.

The League of Notions

The Cabaret in the Woods, circa 1918.

The Cannon Ball roller coaster front entrance - 1919 season. Here she is - there she goes!

The fairly unknown Cannon Ball coaster was built in 1919 for concessionaire Fred Pearce.

Laugh Your Troubles Away

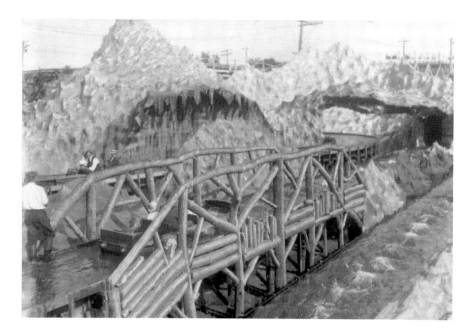

The Rapids Gorge water ride as seen in the late teens.

Frisco's Underworld was a walk through San Francisco's Chinatown.

The interior of the Frisco's Underworld walk-through, late teens.

The War Years

The Goat Ride, located near the Whip, was another popular children's attraction.

The What is It? attraction was located next to the Big Dipper. When is it? Probably around 1919.

81

The Smile attraction, circa 1920. "Smile Dam you Smile"

Lining up for the Shoot-the-Chutes, circa 1917.

The War Years

The Navy First attraction, presented by the US Navy in 1917. "Enlist Now!"

A post-WWI view of the Shoot-the-Chutes. Note the biplane shaped cars on the Aero-stat at left.

CHAPTER EIGHT
THE ROARING TWENTIES

Aerial view of the Marine Causeway, taken around 1924 from the top of the Shoot-the-Chutes.

The park expanded to 156 acres in 1920, and brought the addition of three more rides. Riverview purchased a new 180-foot Ferris Wheel made by the Shaw Construction Company, an unknown type of ride called the Skedaddle, and the Big Dipper coaster, later renamed the Zephyr and the Comet. The Big Dipper was a standard type of John Miller coaster that Miller called the "Deep Dipper" model, because of the drops going all the way to the ground. The coaster had seventeen dips in all. The new ride was a smash hit, and grossed $115,000 for its first season. In

1936, the Big Dipper was renamed the Zephyr when the coaster trains were covered in stainless steel and styled to look like the fashionable, Burlington Zephyr streamlined locomotives.

According to George Schmidt's son, William B. Schmidt, in a paper presented in December, 1941, to the National Association of Amusement Parks, the park began working on the idea of covering the trains after three people were killed while standing up on the park's coasters in 1935. Two were killed on the Big Dipper and one on the Skyrocket. The paper further claims that the covered trains premiered for the 1938 season. However, it appears that Mr. Schmidt may have been mistaken when he wrote that paper. Newspaper reports state that the steel-covered trains made their debut in 1936 on the Big Dipper, when it was renamed Zephyr, and on the Skyrocket, when it was renamed Blue Streak. According to George Hunt, the ride manager of the Comet from 1947-1963, Riverview ran cloth-covered trains on the Pippin in 1934 and 1935 at the request of the park's insurance company. This experimentation was logical as the Big Dipper killed a rider who stood up on the ride in July 1932. Since the Schmidts were very safety-minded, it appears that they were trying to find a way to prevent injuries. Riverview was one of the few parks in the nation to use covered trains.

Riverview's Shaw Wheel, with the Derby coaster at rear, 1920 season.

The construction of the Big Dipper (aka Zephyr and Comet), winter of 1919-1920.

Another view of the new Big Dipper entrance and the rest of the midway, 1920.

The loading platform of the Big Dipper roller coaster, 1920.

The Big Dipper's first drop. Note the dense foliage covering the drop. You won't see that on many coasters these days!

The front of the Big Dipper (aka Zephyr and Comet) roller coaster, 1920 season.

The Big Dipper coaster crew, 1920.

The Roaring Twenties

The rear turnaround on the Big Dipper (aka Zephyr and Comet) roller coaster.

Workers installing the "old woman riding a dipper" atop the Big Dipper coaster entrance, 1920.

Laugh Your Troubles Away

Looking north up the Bowery around 1921. At left is the Jack Rabbit, at center the entrance to the Greyhound coaster, to the right is Puzzle Town and the Ferris Wheel. The roller coaster in the background is the Derby.

The Noah's Ark funhouse was one of the new attractions for the 1920 season.

Looking down the Bowery, circa 1920. The rides from left to right are the Greyhound coaster (aka Gee Whiz), the Eye-Full Tower, the Derby coaster, the Ferris Wheel, and the Ginger Snap.

One of Riverview's Wheel of Fortune games that had to be removed in the 20's after public protest. This building was originally the Velvet Coaster loading station and later an arcade.

Riverview's parking garage, 1921.

Young Alligator Joe's Alligator and Ostrich Farm, mid to late 1920's.

Does Crime Pay? Russell's Penitentiary Portrayal.

How good folks go bad for only twenty cents. Scenes taken in the early 20's.

Laugh Your Troubles Away

A rocking funhouse known as Noah's Ark was also introduced in 1920. The building was shaped like an Ark and rocked back and forth, just as if it were riding waves. Many animal figures decorated the exterior of the Ark. Inside were various funhouse stunts such as moving stairs, animated figures, and rotating barrels. Some new funhouse stunts were also added to the Bug House for 1920 to keep patrons coming back to that attraction as well.

Chicago's mayor, William "Big Bill" Thompson, held the first of his annual Schoolkids Days on May 24th, 1920. He distributed free passes to children converged on the park for an entire day with their classmates. In 1922 and 1923, women's groups forced Mayor Thompson to stop his Schoolkids Days by complaining that he corrupted youth by closing school for the day. They also charged that children as young as eight were lingering in the park until 10pm, spending money on gambling games or in the penny arcades which were "filthy and indecent". Mrs.

Joseph Bowen, president of the Women's City Club, claimed that "A visit to Riverview was not an educational matter." Mayor Thompson responded, "My answer to her is that during the first year of my holidays for the school childrn at Riverview, 250,000 copies of the Constitution were put into the children's hands. The second year, 287,000 histories of the live of George Washington were given out. And last year, 518,000 brief histories of the life of Abraham Lincoln were given to the children. The increased attendance shows that the parents are satisfied". Luckily for the kids, Chicago Alderman, Charlie Weber, took over the sponsorship and continued the outings until his death in 1960.

Mayor Thompson was a very good friend to Riverview. According to Al Griffin, writing in the Spring 1975 issue of Chicago History, Thompson prevented the park from becoming a battleground for the Capone and O'Banion gangs in the mid-twenties. Griffin says that the bootleggers fought

The news media gathered for the launch of the expedition ship "Big Bill", 1924. Note the movie camera at far right.

The Roaring Twenties

Immediately after the launch of the "Big Bill", 1924.

to supply beer for the 50,000 - 75,000 Germans who attended the park on the weekend, in spite of Prohibition. The gangs shot up each other's speakeasies all around the park's perimeter. Mayor Thompson made it clear to both sides that they were to stay out of Riverview.

The park's big musical for the 1920 season was Emile De Recat's Stop! Look! Loosen!," which was presumedly a parody of the 1915 Broadway hit, "Stop! Look! Listen!". Other general improvements to the parks grounds were scheduled as well. New buildings replaced old ones. New concrete walks with a covering of "Tarvia" (ashphalt) were installed, thereby eliminating dust. A new bottling plant and ice-making plant supplied thirsty patrons during the warm summer months.

Many new attractions opened for the 1921 season. The Pippin roller coaster, better known as the Silver Flash or The Flash, was the main

attraction. Norm Cherry remembers, "The Flash had permanent handles on the back of each seat, unlike a lap bar on most coasters. I remember being pulled out of my seat, especially when riding the last seat."

Designed by John Miller, the ride proved popular, but a horrible accident took place in July 1937. A broken cotter key caused a wheel to release, causing the train to fail to climb a hill and then roll back and get stuck in a dip. The brakeman controlling the following train failed to stop it in time and the two trains collided. In all, twenty-two people were injured. In 1938, Riverview equipped the ride with covered trains like those already used on the Zephyr and Blue Streak. Rather than cover the Pippin trains, the old Jack Rabbit trains were covered with stainless-steel instead. The name changed to Silver Flash, and the ride's entrance was completely redone. Also installed was an automatic inter-locking block signal system which insured that two trains would never collide again.

Another new ride for 1921 included the open Dodge-Em cars in which drivers attempted to keep from bumping into other cars. Unlike modern bumper cars, these early model Dodge-Em's steering wheels turned the car in the opposite direction from which the driver turned, almost guaranteeing that riders would collide with another vehicle. Also installed was an Aerojoy Plane ride where riders controlled the sail of the suspended tub they rode in as it circled a central mast. The sail swiveled the tub in and out from the mast. It was very similar to a later ride from a different manufacturer known as the Flying Scooters.

The Pippin originally ran these 3 car, 4 benches per car trains when it opened in 1921.

A walk-through maze called Puzzle Town and a Pony ride for the kiddies, with 50 ponies, were also new for that year. The Thousand Islands ride became the Mill on the Floss with the addition of a paddle wheel and a new pumping system by the Miller and Baker Company. Miller and Baker also designed the building that the Dodge-Em's were placed in. Emile De Recat again presented the season's big musical Smiles of 1921. Late night firework shows named, "Fort Dearborn Massacre", Great Chicago Fire, and "Le Grand Fete da Fea (Festival of Fire)" were presented around the July Fourth holiday.

The Pippin roller coaster construction, 1921.

The Roaring Twenties

The Pippin roller coaster right after construction, 1921. Note that Lane Tech High School has not been built yet.

The Pippin roller coaster taken around 1930. Lane Tech High School is now in background.

Laugh Your Troubles Away

In 1922, no new rides were built, but the Evans and Gordan Famous Collection of Freak Animals made its debut. The show featured such animals as a four-horned goat, an eight-legged horse, a three-legged steer, and siamese twin calves, all for a seventeen cent admission charge. The park began to shrink in total acreage to 148, down from 156 the previous year. The reason for the shrinkage appears to be the encroachment of the City of Chicago on the park property through street widenings and the addition of a streetcar turnaround on Western Avenue. It is a trend that continued throughout the remainder of the park's life. George Schmidt, the park manager, also

The first Dodge-em cars, a new attraction for 1921.

The Dodge-em building, seen here shortly after construction, 1921.

The Roaring Twenties

created the National Association Of Amusement Parks (N.A.A.P) that year. This group continues to this day as the International Association of Attractions and Amusement Parks (I.A.A.P.A.).

In November of 1922, John Miller drew plans for a new roller coaster he called The Speeder, perhaps

based on his standard Speed-O-Plane coaster series. This proposed coaster was to be funded by stockholder Mr. Merle and his Associates and was to occupy the site of the Royal Gorge Scenic Railway. However, Riverview rejected the design and another one based on Miller's newest coaster line, the Deep-Dips, was created.

The Puzzle Town walk-through, 1921. "Johny get a monkey wrench, Fathers a nut!"

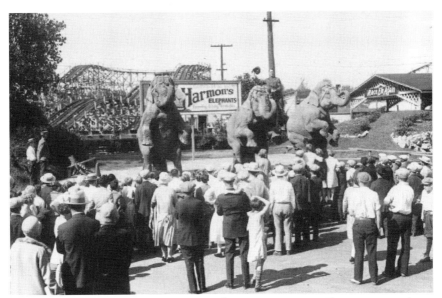

Harmon's Elephants performing at the free Circus, 1926. The coaster at the rear is the Jack Rabbit.

The children's pony ride, 1921.

Riverview's Pony Ride delighted the youngsters!

Converting the Thousand Islands ride into Mill on the Floss, 1921.

The Mill on the Floss loading platform, circa 1921.

Laugh Your Troubles Away

The year 1923 finally saw the construction and opening of Miller's ride, the Skyrocket roller coaster. In 1936, the Skyrocket was renamed Blue Streak when the original trains were covered with steel. The ride was later remodeled into the Fireball in 1959.

Races began at 8:30pm with six races every night. Sunday soccer games were played in the infield area of the Motordrome the following year.

The removal of the Sinking of the Titanic building and the first Blue Streak roller coaster took place in 1924 and the classic Bobs roller

The Skyrocket (aka Blue Streak, Fireball) entrance, 1923.

The Caterpillar ride, a circular track ride which surprised patrons by covering them with a canopy during the middle of the ride, and Dr.Browning's Curiosities, which featured an assortment of freak animals, appeared in 1923. It is likely that Dr. Browning purchased his curiosities from Evans-Gordan who had that "wonderful zoo" the year before. This year also saw the use of the Motordrome property as a greyhound racing track.

coaster was built on the land they formerly occupied. George Schmidt visited Ocean Park, California in 1923, and noticed a new type of roller coaster designed by the firm of Prior and Church. Thomas W. Prior and Frederick A. Church, had met at Riverview Park and become business partners.

The Roaring Twenties

The Skyrocket, as seen from outside the gates.

The Skyrocket (aka Blue Streak & Fireball) roller coaster entrance and midway, opening season of 1923. The Pippin (aka Silver Flash and Flash) entrance is at right.

Happy kids on the Caterpillar ride, 1923.

The new Caterpillar ride for 1923. Notice the well-dressed African-Americans in the foreground at left.

Evans and Gordon's Famous Collection of Freak Animals, 1921.

In 1918, Thomas Prior died, and his son Frank took his place in the partnership. After operating rides at the Venice Pier in California for a number of years, Fred and Frank eventually contracted with John Miller to design a new coaster, the Venice Pier Big Dipper. According to coaster historian Mike Chew, John Miller and Fred Church apparently talked about possible improvements to roller coaster trains during the design discussions for the Big Dipper.

Miller and Church filed patents for improved coaster trains within days of each other in 1923. Both Miller's and Church's coaster trains had articulated couplings that enabled them to run on a wildly twisting and curving track. While each patent was different, they were similar enough that Miller thought that it was a theft of his ideas and ceased working with Church. Miller also persued the issue with his patent attorney who

informed him that there was no violation of his patent.

Church took his newly designed trains and set about making some very distinctive coasters for the 1920's. Schmidt decided to purchase one for Riverview and the Bobs quickly became the most popular ride in the park. Noted for its high speed and swooping turns, a ride on this coaster was never to be forgotten. One ad from the first season boldly claimed that the Bobs had been "specially built to amuse bobbed-haired girlies." Norm Cherry states that the Bobs was, "The absolute best ride in the park, especially the last seat. You could ride again for 25 cents. I remember one night riding six times in a row, beating the record among my friends. Once I mentioned the Bobs while visiting Coney Island, New York. They all had great respect for Riverview's Bobs. Chicago pride!"

Laugh Your Troubles Away

The Bobs' ride manager, Carl Jeske, had a collection of 60,000 lost earrings that earned him a place in Ripley's Believe It Or Not. Jeske claimed that all the earrings had been found underneath the Bobs and no two were duplicates. However, former employee, Ralph Lopez, stated that other ride managers donated jewelry lost on their rides to Jeske's collection. The Bobs was the most popular and profitable ride in the park and on busy days, three trains rode on the track to accommodate the crowds.

George Schmidt used the success of Riverview's Bobs to try to sell Prior and Church Bobs coasters to other parks. According to Prior and Church's

Bobs - King of Coasters promotional brochure, George Schmidt and Riverview's Secretary Al Hodge were two of only four sales agents for Prior and Church. The others were Traver Engineering, and the L. A. Thompson Company. Schmidt actively wrote other parks trying to get them to purchase one. He also permitted prospective buyers to examine Riverview's Bobs after-hours and even off-season to see if it would be suitable for their parks, too. A 1925 letter from Al Hodge to Brady McSwigan of Pittsburgh's Kennywood Park regarding the Bobs has survived all these years. Hodge asks that if McSwigan decides to "give us a fling at a Bobs in Kennywood, let me know before we get too many contracts for next

Dr. Browning's Curiosities, an animal freak show from 1923, stands near the Casino (left at rear).

Constructing the Bobs roller coaster, Winter 1924.

The Grecian columned front entrance of the Bobs roller coaster, 1924.

One of the most dramatic Bobs pictures ever - at the top of the first drop!

year as the indications are that we are going to be up to our necks with new rides by the time the fall season rolls around." Sadly, Kennywood never purchased one, preferring to stay with John Miller designed coasters throughout the 1920's. Hodge did convince one or more of the Kennywood principles to purchase stock with him in the Coney Island Coaster Company, which erected a Bobs coaster in New York. This coaster was later known as the Tornado until its destruction in three fires between December 1977 and January 1978.

The Bobs has been the subject of much debate among roller coaster enthusiasts. How high was it? How fast did it go? Who built it? It appears that the blueprints for the ride are contradictory. The lift hill was built at 54 feet, nine inches high and period photos show it about that height. The

ride was revised over the years and numbers ranging from 65 to 77 feet appear on some surviving blueprints. The slope of the first drop was 46 degrees at construction, although that too may have been steeper if the lift hill height was increased. The top speed was approximately 45 - 50 miles per hour at the bottom of the first drop. It may have seemed faster to riders who were thrown around the car during one of the sixteen hills or twelve curves, but it really wasn't. The length of the ride, 3,235 feet, took two minutes and 33 seconds to traverse.

Much has also been made of Harry G. Traver's involvement in the construction of the Bobs. Initially, it was thought that Traver designed it, since he was an honored pioneer in the amusement ride industry. However, the surviving

The Roaring Twenties

original blueprints identify the rightful designer as Fred Church. An August of 1924 Billboard article states that Traver Engineering was responsible for the construction of the Bobs. Traver's close affiliation with the firm of Prior and Church as a sales agent allowed him to be the preferred construction contractor for many of the Bobs coasters that were built. Coasters were usually constructed in those days with a supervisor, a foreman, and perhaps a couple of hand picked workers, with the rest of the construction crew raised locally. Traver's firm may have brought the supervisory skill, while the Belmont Construction Company or the North West Roller Coaster Construction Company, owned by George Schmidt, provided the rest of the labor.

Traver's actual involvement in the Bobs construction is still a question mark. Prior & Church were too busy with Bobs construction projects in Southern California to oversee it themselves, but it was of paramount importance to them that the Riverview installation be built correctly, utilizing Church's construction techniques. This would be Church's first coaster in the East Coast marketplace and since Chicago was the site of the newly formed National Association Of Amusement Parks (N.A.A.P) annual convention, the Bobs was certain to be seen by other park managers. Although it's possible that Fred Church

came to Riverview to supervise construction, Mike Chew believes that Riverview's own builder, Bill Gierke, traveled to California in late 1923 or early 1924 to learn the patented Church method of track construction. Gierke then returned to Riverview to build the Bobs, and may even be the one who taught Church's methods to Traver. Although Riverview's business ledger for 1924 is currently unavailable to tell us whether any monies were paid to Traver, the authors believe that there is support for Chew's theory.

First, Traver's name does not appear anywhere on the Bobs blueprints, unlike other Church designed coasters whose blueprints still exist. Second, Gierke is cited in Billboard magazine as being "the genius builder at Riverview" and is known to have supervised the construction of the Detroit Palace Gardens Bobs coaster which opened in 1925. Third, the announcement of

Rounding the rear turnaround on the Bobs roller coaster, 1924. The Riverview staff called this turn the Horseshoe.

Laugh Your Troubles Away

The Bobs front turn, taken in 1924.

Traver's involvement in the Riverview Bobs didn't come until three months after it opened. It was only then that Traver Engineering was given credit for building the Bobs and was now available to build Bobs coasters for others. The Billboard story may have been planted to give Traver the industry credibility for future Bobs coaster construction projects. As Mike Chew states, "Traver was never shy talking up his business projects. So why not a peep out of him during the construction of the Riverview Bobs? Was he afraid the ride might not work and his reputation might be damaged? Or was there another explanation?"

Prior and Church continued to design Bobs coasters for Riverview for the next eight years. They proposed a new 2000 foot long Bobs in 1925, but its short length allowed only two trains to run at once and it was rejected. Riverview's popularity in the Twenties required rides that could accomodate a

large number of riders per hour, which was why Riverview's coasters needed to be long enough to accommodate three trains running simultaneously. In 1926, a proposed larger Bobs was drawn up for the site of the Jack Rabbit. This design was made in both 3000 and 3250 foot long versions. For reasons unknown, these coasters were again rejected. A final attempt to sell Riverview another Bobs was made in January, 1932, with a 2550 foot version of the 1926 proposal. By then however, the Great Depression made building a new coaster impossible.

The next few years brought few extravagant rides to the park. In 1925, the Santa Fe Miniature Railway was installed by the real-life Santa Fe Railroad Company as a promotion, a wax museum with historical figures of Lenin, Trotsky, and Germany's ex-President Hindenburg, and display of a man-ape. The man-ape was advertised as a mute, who

A little girl posing on the Santa Fe Miniature Railway, 1925.

came directly from Africa's jungles. He was exhibited in a steel-bound arena located on the park's riverfront. The ads urged patrons to learn and study evolution by viewing the man-ape. Most likely, the poor man-ape was a mute, circus freak being exploited to cash in on the interest in the theory of evolution. Sometime during 1925, park founder Wilhelm (William) Schmidt passed away and his son, George, assumed the Presidency of the Riverview Park Company in addition to his duties as General Manager of the park.

A new Kiddy Land, located next to the Bobs opened in 1926. Included was a Kiddy Bobs coaster which had a horsehead on the front car of each of the trains. The original blueprints show that the trains were designed to have had two horse heads instead of one, but the second head was eliminated to save both cost and weight. The Kiddy Bobs was designed by

Prior & Church, designers of the larger Bobs and it was very thrilling for a Kiddy coaster.

Unfortunately, the Kiddy Bobs was removed when the rest of Kiddy Land was relocated next to the Shoot-the-Chutes in 1935. The reason for the relocation was to make room for the newly acquired Flying Turns ride.

Painting the Kiddie Bobs coaster trains, 1926.

Laugh Your Troubles Away

The Kiddy Bobs roller coaster entrance, 1926.

These gorgeous models are promoting the new (Mother Goose's Own) Kiddy Land, 1926.

The Roaring Twenties

The Kiddy Bobs roller coaster, just stopped on the brake run, 1926.

Two models posing on a Kiddy circle swing in Kiddy Land, 1926.

The Kiddy Bobs coaster rounding a curve, 1926.

The newly complete Kiddie Bobs train, 1926.

The Roaring Twenties

Around 1926, Riverview hosted a Light Airplane Show. Various small plane manufacturers brought examples of their planes to display around the park. To tie in with this, the park arranged for some Lisk flight trainers that the public could fly. Publicity photos were snapped with flappers posed on a extra-large trainer, while the other "flying machines" were scattered around the park. Exactly how long they remained in the park is unknown, but the last known Light Airplane Show took place in 1931, so the trainers may have stayed until then.

The Riverview Light Airplane Show, circa 1926.

The Lisk flight trainers that allowed the public to fly, circa 1926.

Laugh Your Troubles Away

A promotional picture for the Lisk Flight Trainers stationed at various places in the park, circa 1926.

This new bi-plane shaped car replaced the original ones on the Aero-Stat (aka Strat-O-Stat).

An elaborate flower shop and pet store was built for 1926 that featured a marble fountain which sprayed water on a school of goldfish in a pool with colored lights. In addition to flower arrangements, one could purchase singing canaries, love birds, puppies, and African monkeys there.

A free Circus was brought in to perform at various locations around the park such as the Carousel, the Whip, the Shoot-the-Chutes, and Jack Rabbit.

A "drink on a stick" was the new rage at the concession counter. Today, these creations are called popsicles. The Winner ride was removed and replaced with a bicycle rental. The Shoot-the-Chutes had new electric lights installed and the Mill on the Floss purchased new mountain scenery.

The Roaring Twenties

A spectacular Electric Fountain with a "Living Tableaux" (e.g., young women in bathing suits posing on it) was built near the Shoot-The-Chutes in 1927. Initially, the fountain was a ticketed attraction, but in 1930 it became a free show. In the later years of the park, the Electric Fountain stood rusting because supposedly only the two concessionaires who built it knew how to operate it. To save money on expensive union musicians, Riverview installed an "Auditorium Orthophonic" in the ballroom. This was a record player especially made by Victor for use in large public places. At the end of the 1927 season, Riverview proclaimed that it had its best season in history, largely due to good, warm weather!

The Electric Fountain with its Living Tableaux in action.

Construction of the Electric Fountain, 1927.

Laugh Your Troubles Away

The Electric Fountain, 1927. The two men in front are believed to be the concessionaires.

The Tilt-A-Whirl building, pictured in 1928. If you look closely, you can still see the faded paint on the canopy advertising the Cycle Whiz, a bicycle concession.

In 1928, the Tilt-A-Whirl made its debut at Riverview. It was placed in the building formerly occupied by the Winner ride and bicycle concession. Tilt-A-Whirl's, made in Minnesota, can still be found today at fairs, carnivals, and some amusement parks. The park ads also now listed the total park acreage at 142, down from 148 in 1922.

Two dapper ladies about to enjoy a ride on the Tumble Bug, circa 1928.

Waiting for the Tumble Bug ride to start, circa 1930.

CHAPTER NINE

THE DEPRESSION YEARS

The River Walk after the installation of the Flying Turns in 1935.

The Stock Market Crash of 1929 and the onset of the Great Depression greatly reduced the amount of money available for new attractions. Park advertising slogans represented the mood of the country with such mottos as "The Happy Hunting Ground for all who hunt happiness" and "Chase the blues - come to Riverview." During the thirties, the park lost additional acreage with the sale of property to the City of Chicago for the construction of Lane Tech High School. Legend has it that the park did not want to sell the land for the new High School and was pressured into it by the City. Only a few major attractions were added during this turbulent period. New for 1931 was the purchase of a Traver Engineering Laugh-In-The-Dark Jr. ride. Riverview named it Spook Town and included lots of Halloween type figures and effects inside. This ride was later revamped and renamed Ghost Train in 1956.

In April 1932, just before the new season opened, some workmen re-tarring a roof accidently started a massive blaze. Firefighters ran hoses to the park's lagoon and drained it of water fighting the flames. The fire totally destroyed the Bug House, and heavily damaged the Derby Racer, which was removed after reconstruction costs were deemed too high. Universal Pictures filmed the firemen extinguishing the flames, so it could be shown in movie theaters across the country as part of the weekly newsreel. This footage can be seen in the video companion to this book, Laugh Your Troubles Away - The Complete History of Riverview Park. Supposedly, the undamaged wood from the Derby Racer and the Jack Rabbit, which wasn't damaged in the fire, was used to repair the park's other coasters throughout the Depression. The popular Aladdin's Castle funhouse was constructed to replace the Bug House. According to legend, the park had been working on plans for Aladdin's Castle before the fire so constructing a

The Spook Town dark ride premiered in 1931.

Laugh Your Troubles Away

Aladdin's Castle may have been the most distinctive funhouse ever built.

new funhouse so quickly was not as big a problem as it could have been. The original blueprints for the building, drawn by engineer Julius Floto, call it Bluebeard's Castle, so evidently the park desired a less scary name.

Being a funhouse, Aladdin's Castle had many of the usual features that other funhouses across the country had - mirrored rooms, slanted floors, pitch-black passages, air jets in the stairs, slides, a rotating barrel to try and run through, etc. What made Aladdin's Castle unique was the elaborate facade that looked like an Arabian fortress, with a huge portrait of Aladdin himself gracing the front entrance. How could a visitor to Riverview not want to go in? Norm Cherry tells us of his experiences there, "I remember being lost inside the castle. I must have been five or six years old and even with a parent in tow, managed to get lost! I remember years later taking the barrel ride down at the end of the walk".

Advertising for this season was aimed at preventing people from spending less in anticipation of the 1933 Chicago World's Fair. The ad copy read -

"A World's Fair of Thrills" and "Time To Play Will Always Pay." Another interesting promotion for Riverview was its display of Rockne 6 automobiles right inside the front gate. With six new Rockne 6's, and a huge display sign, Riverview helped Studebaker promote its short-lived vehicle, named after the famous Notre Dame football coach Knute Rockne.

For the 1933 Season, Riverview remodeled its Over The Falls ride building into the Hell 'n' Back funhouse. By 1940, it was renamed Hades. With the 1933 Chicago World's Fair in town, Riverview found itself in stiff competition for its patrons' scarce money. After all, the Depression was still on and the Fair beckoned to Riverview's regular patrons. To meet the competition head on, Riverview first tried to increase its advertising, which had been scarce the previous years. Ads told of a new FREE pageant called A Century of Nonsense, which was a parody of the World's Fair theme A Century of Progress. This tactic was not entirely successful. Riverview stayed open, but it was hurting.

The Depression Years

The Flying Turns ride offered great thrills!

Since the Fair was still there in 1934, something had to be done. The answer was Riverview's famous "Two Cent Days and Five Cent Nights." Gate admission was reduced to two cents on Tuesday afternoons from noon to five, and five cents from six until closing on Mondays and Friday evenings. Ads also told readers to "Ask Neighborhood Merchants For Free Tickets." These new promotions worked much better and definitely gave Riverview some relief from the Depression.

For the 1935 season, the park purchased the Flying Turns roller coaster and the "banjo" style lights from the 1933-1934 Chicago World's Fair. The Flying Turns was a unique coaster ride where the cars traveled freely in a wooden trough instead of on top of a track. The designer, Norman Bartlett, intended to give the rider a sensation of flight, which explains why the cars were shaped like biplanes. Many Riverview patrons thought the ride was more like a bobsled ride. Riverview originally

Laugh Your Troubles Away

The Riverview Roller Club, posed for a picture in the 1930's.

had wanted to purchase a Flying Turns in 1931, shortly after the ride's introduction. Unfortunately, Riverview wanted a three year exclusive on the ride and apparently they could not raise the money required and were forced to wait and purchase a used one. The ride was very successful financially and lasted until the demise of the park in 1967. Also moved from the World's Fair was the Motordrome attraction, where stunt motorcycle riders performed in a circular wooden building.

Another new attraction for 1935 was a Bisch-Rocco Flying Scooters ride where riders could "fly" their own car by moving a small rudder attached to the front. This allowed riders to control how high or low the car went while the ride spun around. According to George Schmidt, who wrote a testimonial as to how great the ride was, Riverview received the very first Flying Scooters ride manufactured. The park purchased two Big Eli No. 16 Ferris wheels that were set up side by side. Although some have claimed

that this Double Ferris Wheel had a single axle to support two wheels, it is clear from film of the wheels that they are two independent rides that were set up next to one another to facilitate loading.

In 1936, a new attraction, Midget Auto Racing, was added to the Riverview speedway for patrons to watch, along with a new ride to complement it, the Indianapolis Race Track. Located between the Bobs and the Flying Turns, the track gave riders the chance to drive their own "race car" in safety.

The Comet front viewed around 1940.

The Depression Years

The biggest attraction for 1936 was the conversion of the Eye-full Tower to the Pair-O-Chutes parachute drop. The ride was patterned after a parachute training tower invented by Major James H. Strong. Riders sat in small wooden seats that were suspended from the arms of the tower and hoisted up, way into the sky. Once released from the top, the rider was in free fall until air filled the parachute to slow the descent. Norm Cherry recalls, "I remember the feeling of your stomach in your throat when being dropped from 200 feet. Also, you never really knew when your seat was going to be released. It added to the anxiety of it all".

Testing the Pair-O-Chutes prior to opening, 1936. Notice the full hoop that is around the parachute edge. This was later removed after being shown to be unnecessary.

In June of 1939, a couple married on the ride. The bride's sister, Louise Pittman, wrote the authors in 1994 about her experiences that day, but unfortunately she did not provide the couple's names. Mrs. Pittman describes that day...

I was eleven years old in 1939 - and the thought of my older sister getting married was exciting enough - but she was going to get married at Riverview Park! The day finally came - having no car, the family took the streetcar that ran on South Chicago Avenue to the park.

It was very hot that day - perfect weather for an outdoor wedding - it turned out to reach 90 degrees that day. So many people were crowded by the new parachute ride. There were three chutes; my sister and husband-to-be were in the front chute, while the bridesmaids occupied the two rear chutes. As the chutes started to go up slowly, the pastor, who was standing at a microphone at the base of the ride, asked them the marriage vows. When all was completed the chutes came down - how exciting it all was! During the ceremony, an elderly woman fainted from the heat of the day. My sister learned of it and promptly went to visit the lady and gave her the wedding bouquet.

After the wedding, the family and bride and groom and guests went to a church to renew their vows, and then on to the wedding reception. What an exciting day - I'll never forget! Thanks to my sister I wore the very same dress at my wedding in 1946. Thanks to the owners of Riverview for that exciting time!

Laugh Your Troubles Away

The wedding on the Pair-O-Chutes took place in 1939.

This young couple was married on the Pair-O-Chutes in June, 1939. Courtesy of the Chicago Historical Society ICHi-20025.

After seeing Riverview's Pair-O-Chutes, the 1939 New York World's Fair decided to construct a larger one for their entertainment midway. That tower still stands silently today, looking over the deserted section of Coney Island that once was Steeplechase Park. It was recently inspected and found to be in excellent shape. Repainted bright red, it is sealed against the elements. Some local Coney Island residents hope it will reopen someday, although prospects look dim now that the New York Mets have announced the move of their Class A farm team to a new stadium to be built on that site. The stadium would open for the year 2000 season and current plans call for the Parachute tower to remain standing, just beyond the right field foul pole.

The new ride for 1937 was a Cuddle-Up. People sat in little round tubs that spun as they moved along a large double figure-eight pattern in the floor. That same year, 1937, is believed to be the year that the park built new rocketship-shaped cars for the Aero-Stat, and renamed the ride Strat-O-Stat. Riverview also purchased an Octopus ride for 1938. The Octopus is a spinning ride with six arms that have buckets attached in clusters of two at each end. Each bucket cluster turned freely. Riders loved it because as the ride spun, the arms went up and down and the buckets spun too.

The unusual Boomerang ride was installed in Riverview by concessionaire R. Curland in 1939. Riders tubs were attached to a rotating platform, brought up to high speed, and then detached from the platform and sent flying down a tunnel to the end of the ride. The park's water rides received a sprucing up in 1939 with the addition of eleven new Mill On The Floss boats and eight new Shoot-The-Chutes boats.

The big new attraction for in 1940 was a 84-foot double Ferris Wheel named the Sky Wheel by the manufacturer and called the Sky Ride by Riverview. The Sky Wheel was really two Ferris Wheels, one on top of the other. They are supported by giant steel arms which turn the entire structure as the wheels revolve. Very few Sky Wheels are left in parks today, although a few can be seen with traveling carnivals. A historical note regarding this particular ride - a 1983 Amusement Business article says that a primitive prototype of the ride was installed at Riverview in 1938, while the manufacturer's advertisement for the ride gives the date as 1939. The 1940 date is based on information furnished to Billboard at the beginning of the 1940 season. It may represent either the date the prototype was updated or simply the date the park chose to begin actively promoting the ride.

The rocket ship-shaped cars for the Strat-O-Strat were designed by the Humphrey Company, the owners of Euclid Beach Park in Cleveland. Riverview obtained the plans and constructed them in their own shops. Photo courtesy of Walter Schaeffer.

Laugh Your Troubles Away

Other rides added for 1940 included the Streamline Pacific miniature train, a Moon Rocket, and a Roll-O-Plane. The Moon Rocket was a flat ride in which a train of bullet-shaped cars travelled counter-clockwise around a circular, banked track. The Roll-O-Plane consisted of a long rotating arm with cylindrical pods at each end that the riders sat in. Each pod could be rotated 360 degrees by the riders if they so chose. It was not a ride for those prone to stomach upset!

Another new park feature was the Magic Trees lighting system. This system allowed each tree trunk in the Hippodrome section of the park to glow with a soft, indirect shade of pastel. The Magic Trees system was developed by electrical engineer Art Cleary and perfected with help from William B. Schmidt. To complete the update, neon lights were added to the ride facades.

A woman posing on the Man in the Moon in Riverview's photo studio.

The Palace of Wonders magic/freak show. Photo taken about 1935.

Sitting in the Flash's new covered trains.

Launching the new covered trains for the Flash Coaster.

The new Flash trains head on.

Laugh Your Troubles Away

A youthful William B. Schmidt posing in his auto about 1929 with his boat, "Miss Riverview" on a trailer. Note the Riverview wheel cover on the running board.

The sleek new Dodge-em cars replaced the early ones in the 1930's.

Promoting the 1932 Rockne 6 automobile at Riverview wasn't able to save this car from discontinuation in 1933.

Another view of the Rockne 6 promotion, 1932.

Laugh Your Troubles Away

The Big Dipper, seen here in the later part of the 1930's.

George Schmidt, at the head of the trouble, and his son, William Schmidt at far right, can be seen in this group photo taken in the early 1930's.

132

CHAPTER TEN

POST-WAR RIVERVIEW

Dick "Two-Ton Baker", was Riverview's spokesman for many years.

Since the Depression, 1946 was the first year Riverview had to contend with decreasing attendance. Immediately after the war, people who had been forced to stay in town because of gasoline rationing suddenly got the travel bug. In 1945, Riverview had as many as 12,000 patrons during the day and 18,000 at night. Riverview would not say exactly how many were attending in 1946, but in Schmidt's words it was "hardly 30,000".

In August of 1946, rumors circulated that Riverview would be sold to P.K. Wrigley, of chewing gum fame, to build a new Wrigley Field for his Chicago Cubs baseball team. William Schmidt said, "There is absolutely no truth to it; the park definitely isn't for sale." For his part, Mr. Wrigley commented, "I can assure you I haven't bought Riverview and have no intention of doing so. We have too much money invested in Wrigley Field to make such a move, and we're pretty well satisfied with it." This may have been the first time rumors of Riverview's impending sale surfaced, but it would not be the last.

On August 17, 1946, tragedy struck Riverview as Walter Osta, the 73-year-old manager of the Mill On The Floss, was crushed to death when he fell between a moving boat and the side of the boat channel. Part of the ride operator's job was to check the ride's inner island for patrons who might have gotten out of their boats. Mr. Osta was apparently trying to cross over to the inner island when he slipped and fell.

For the 1946 season, the Bobs was equipped with a new air brake, designed by William Schmidt. Schmidt, always concerned with improving the park's safety, stated that the new system would do three things. First, it put all responsibility of braking and unloading at one location. Second, it

provided a means to stop the trains before the platform, unless the brakes were intentionally released. Finally, it prevented the release of a loaded train from the platform, unless the track section ahead were clear. The Flash was given this same braking system in 1949. The original wooden-bodied Bob's trains were replaced with steel-bodied duplicator. The Bob's rough nature was shaking the wooden cars apart, requiring frequent maintenance.

On December 4, 1946, minority stockholder Henry J. Merle filed a suit calling for the distribution of an alleged $900,000 in undivided profits. To settle the matter, the Riverview Park

A close-up of the Bobs train. Note the plates mounted underneath to keep the train locked to the track.

Company purchased several parcels of land from the estate of Wilhelm (William) A. Schmidt. According to Park Official G. G. Botts, the park had leased these lands from the estate, and "putting all of the land in the ownership of the park corporation would mean more efficient and profitable operation." Since the park corporation no longer had to pay rent to the Schmidt estate, Mr. Merle was satisfied with the use of the money and dropped his lawsuit.

Carl Jeske rides up the hill of the Bobs.

Riverview added new rides every couple of years for the next two decades. The Dive Bomber (also known as a Eyerly Loop-O-Plane) was purchased used in 1943. Loop-O-Planes are still seen today at traveling carnivals, and are often nicknamed "salt and pepper shakers" because they have cylindrical ride buckets. Two arms, each with a bucket attached, spin the rider vertically into a fast diving motion. The Dive Bomber was removed from the park in 1947 or 1948 after an accident occurred, killing two riders. The Roll-O-Plane was moved from the Bowery section of the park to take the Dive Bomber's spot on the midway.

Working on the Bobs.

Laugh Your Troubles Away

The Riverview Scout Train about to pull away. Photo courtesy of George Neisler, Riverview Park Company.

With the end of World War II, the park was able to purchase the Bubble Bounce in 1946 and the famous Riverview Scout & Chief miniature trains for the 1948 season. The Water Bug, a unique ride that had appeared at the 1939 World's Fair in New York, was purchased used and installed by Riverview for the 1948 season. It resembled an aquatic version of the Dodge-ems, with riders driving around a shallow pool in gasoline engine powered boats that used huge rubber inner tubes as bumpers.

During the early 1950's, smaller rides were added along with remodeling and repainting the park. In 1950, Riverview converted their shooting gallery ammunition from BB's to .22 caliber lead bullets. The front portion of the gallery was re-modeled, a canopy added, while the rear portion was rebuilt.

New steel targets and a steel duck tank were purchased from the W. F. Mangels Company in New York.

The Kiddy Tumble Bug ride debuted in 1951. For those who have never seen a Tumble Bug ride, picture a thin, steel track with some small hills on it. As the electric powered cars travel around the track, the also travel up and down the hills, giving roller coaster like thrills. The Mill on the Floss ride became the Tunnel of Love that same year. The new ride for 1952 was the Rotor. This thrill ride spun patrons who stood along the walls at a high speed. Suddenly, the floor dropped out under them pinning them to the wall.

In 1953, the park celebrated the beginning of its 50th season. New for that year was an Atomic Energy exhibit and a radio broadcasting booth. You and the Atom was built by the American Museum of Atomic Energy at Oak Ridge, Tennessee. It featured a 10-foot high model reactor that actually contained a small amount of Uranium-235, which could be used to make a coin radioactive. The visitor's dime was dropped into the reactor, bombarded with neutrons, and then brought up to a Geiger counter to prove its radioactivity. Then it was sealed in plastic and returned to the owner. What a souvenir! Also featured in the display were radioactive turtles and plants. Demonstrations showed the use of tracer atoms in medicine, industry, and agriculture. One section featured information on self-protection in case of nuclear attack.

Riverview considered adding a Kiddy Mill Chute ride this year, patterned after the one at Kennywood Park in Pittsburgh. The original blueprints were lost, so Andy Vettel, Kennywood's extraordinary park maintenance man drew up plans for Riverview. For reasons unknown, Riverview never built the ride.

The Water Bug was like the Dodge-ems, except located in a small pond.

The Greyhound as seen in the 1950's. Photo courtesy of George Neisler, Riverview Park Company.

The Hot Rods racing cars and a strange German ride called the Flying Cars came to the park in 1954. The Hot Rods were miniature autos that anyone could drive and were, as the park told Billboard, "the hottest thing since the Bobs." Norm Cherry recalls, "This was probably every kid's first experience with driving. I remember stalling in the middle of the track and having to be pushed out of harm's way. They gave me another free ride".

The Flying Cars was an unusual device. Riders sat in a automobile-shaped tub which rotated inside a barrel that was 27 feet in diameter. A rider-controlled foot brake allowed the tubs to rotate completely upside-down with the barrel, or just rock back-and-forth at the bottom as the barrel rotated. The operator waited until the ride got up to the top speed of 30 MPH before shouting to the riders, "Put on your brakes"! This ride was removed after an accident where a rider who failed to fasten the lap belt rotated to the top of the barrel and fell out.

Manager George Schmidt began suffering respiratory problems during the early 1950's, and at his doctor's advice, he moved to Palm Springs, California, in September of 1955 to try and get some relief. He suffered a near-fatal bout with pneumonia two months later and on July 3, 1957, he passed away at the age of 72. His son, William Blanxious Schmidt, was promoted from Vice-President to President after his father's death.

Walt Disney opened his now famous California amusement park, Disneyland, in 1955. A little known fact is that Riverview's William Schmidt played a crucial role as an advisor to Disney, along with three managers from other parks. According to the July 30, 1955, edition of Billboard, the other managers were George Whitney, Sr., San Francisco,

Ed Schott, Cincinnati, and Ross Davis, of Los Angeles. At a meeting in 1953, the managers were shown a sketch of Disneyland's layout, and asked to comment. They found major faults with the design, and some of their concerns caused Walt Disney to alter his plans. With some of the group's other comments, Walt simply ignored their advice and did what he wanted. A later Billboard article from June 23, 1958 printed William Schmidt's warning that people need to "investigate before investing" in a theme park. Apparently a rush of people wanted to duplicate the success of Disneyland by haphazardly throwing together theme parks. Indeed, Schmidt was correct in warning the industry because large new theme parks such as Freedomland in New York did close after only a few seasons.

In 1956, Riverview purchased 28 new cars for the Hot Rods, at a cost of $1250 each, and new cars for the Spook Town, which was then renamed Ghost Train. The Rock-O-Plane was removed and the Jet Rocket, a Wedemeyer Super Roto-Jet ride, set in its place. The Showboat came to the park in 1957. The paddlewheel boats traveled around the lagoon and through a new channel dug to the north, but short of the miniature train track.

Added in 1958 was a smaller but popular coaster, the Wild Mouse, which replaced the double Ferris Wheel. Manufactured by Ben Schiff, the Wild Mouse used two person cars that rode along the track quickly and made sharp curves that both delighted and scared riders.

President Harry S. Truman campaigning at Riverview in 1948.

Laugh Your Troubles Away

At a cost of $175,000, the Blue Streak coaster was remodeled into a faster coaster called the Fireball in 1959. Riverview originally intended to raise the lift hill on the coaster to increase the drop. According to one newspaper article, Chicago building authorities cited new building codes that prohibited wooden structures over 35 feet high. Riverview circumvented these regulations by removing the double-dip first drop and placing the drop approximately ten feet underground. The Fireball was famed for being the park's fastest coaster and the park often exaggerated its speed in their advertisements. Speeds of up to 100 miles an hour were claimed. William Schmidt, who had degrees in electrical and mechanical engineering, redesigned the trains himself, adding a feature that caused the lap bars to automatically lock into position as the train left the station.

For 1959, Aladdin's Castle received a new, three-dimensional looking face with eyes that moved, making an already popular funhouse even more distinctive. Riverview also streamlined its operations by leasing the food concessions to the ABC Vending Company, and splitting up the game concessions among a number of different operators. Trying to increase its appeal to teenage dancers, the park hired the host of NBC-TV's "Chicago Bandstand" show, Dave Hull, to DJ its Wednesday night "Date Night Hop". The dance lasted from 7:00pm - 11:00pm at the outdoor bandshell. The "Date Night Hop" admitted couples for free and offered the $5 ride coupon books for $3.50. According to former Chutes Manager Ralph Lopez, "The Date Night Hop never really caught on."

Another 1959 promotion involved the host of WGN radio's "Hi-Fi Club", Wally Phillips. He arrived by helicopter next to the Bobs coaster. Phillips marshalled the Mardi Gras parade at 9:00pm and broadcast live from the park.

The Zephyr Coaster was renamed the Comet around 1940. Here the Comet climbs the lift hill.

Riverview's famous Freak Show lasted until the park closed in 1967. Photo courtesy of Walter Schaeffer.

A busy day in front of the Bobs. Photo courtesy of George Neisler, Riverview Park Co.

CHAPTER ELEVEN

THE TURBULENT SIXTIES

The Hades funhouse was demolished, supposedly due to the land underneath it being eroded by the Chicago River. A new Paratrooper ride emerged in its place. The Safari dark ride replaced the Life show, and a Kiddy Helicopter ride was added for the 1960 season. New for 1961 was a Kiddy Carousel, a Calypso, and a Mountain Road, known elsewhere as the Matterhorn. In 1962, the Cuddle-up was replaced by a smaller version of itself, the brightly painted Crazy Dazy. The $300,000 Space Ride, a Von-Roll manufactured Sky Ride, opened in 1963 after the ride proved its popularity in parks like Disneyland. The Twist arrived in 1964. This ride can be seen in many parks today as the Trabant.

The Space Ride cost $300,000 in 1961. Photo courtesy George Neisler, Riverview Park Company.

The 1965 season saw the removal of the 53-year-old Greyhound coaster and the construction of the Jetstream coaster. The Greyhound had been immaculately maintained over the years and even improved with the addition of air brakes in 1950. However, by the early 1960's, it was clear that a newer coaster was needed to attract more people. The park contacted the Philadelphia Toboggan Company (PTC) to have the ride remodeled, but were convinced that it would cost nearly as much as building a new one. The Jetstream, designed by John Allen, was Riverview's last new ride. Interestingly, the Philadelphia Toboggan Company was trying to get out of the coaster construction business around that time period. So to minimize effort on their part, they sub-contracted the parts sourcing to the National Amusement Device (NAD) company, their rivals in the ride business. The Jetstream featured a 55-foot lift hill and contained about 2,000 feet of track. It also had a new "dead-man" type air-brake system that required an operator to be alert and on duty to keep the brakes open, otherwise they would remain closed. The Jetstream's trains were specially designed by William Schmidt for comfort and safety and were built at the park's machine shops. Many coaster enthusiasts who experienced these trains during the few years that they operated thought them to be more comfortable than the trains offered by PTC or NAD. These trains weighed 11,000 pounds empty and approximately 15,500 pounds with 32 passengers. Since they were heavier than trains avail-

Laugh Your Troubles Away

The Jetstream coaster was Riverview's last new ride. Photo courtesy George Neisler, Riverview Park Company.

able from the other manufacturers, the coaster structure was specially reinforced by designer John Allen to handle up to 55.5 tons. The Jetstream was popular, but the ride never paid back its $303,756.77 construction cost because of the premature closing of the park three seasons later.

The final improvements to the park happened in the last two years. The Dodgem building was remodeled, 60 new European cars replaced the old Dodgems, and the ride was renamed Bump 'Em for 1966. A small change to the Jetstream for the '66 season added fifteen more feet of track to the brake run before the station. The Comet had one of its three trains removed, and one car from the removed train was added to the other two trains. Removing one train increased safety as it was difficult to run three trains on such a short ride, and making remaining trains longer helped to

offset the loss of ride capacity.

In 1967, Riverview debuted its newly renovated carousel after nearly two years of work. In July of 1965, William Schmidt wrote to PTC describing the poor condition of the 1908 carousel and asking them to do a restoration. PTC sent an expert to Chicago who completely disassembled the ride, and inspected every piece to see if it was suitable to be reused. PTC also suggested the park use local artists to repaint the horses, and the park ended up hiring a local company to do the work. The carousel mechanism was rebuilt by PTC and due to the carousel's original design, the replacement gearing slowed the carousel down. The carousel building was given a new sign and the park claimed that it had cost $100,000 total for the restoration work.

The Turbulent Sixties

At the end of the 1967 season, it was suddenly announced that Riverview would close. In interviews with the local papers, the Schmidt family denied that the park would close, but close it did. It happened so quickly that the park employees did not even find out until they punched out at the time clock the last day of operation. "I was punching out to go home, and the assistant Superintendent of the park, Bill Frank, was in the time shanty, and he told me the park was sold," said Chutes manager, Ralph Lopez. "When I got home from work, I heard on the news they were going to tear it down. When I got to work the next day, I didn't know what to do."

The people of Chicago poured out their hearts in letters to the local papers. A good example is this letter from the Aurora Beacon-News: "Taking Riverview away is like telling little children Santa Claus will never come again, or that there is no such thing as make believe, or just telling people you cannot laugh or have fun anymore." The citizens were stunned. Why had their beloved park closed? Rumors flew everywhere. Was it losing money? Did racial tensions hasten its demise? Did the Schmidts just get tired of running it? Some rumors even had the mayor's office forcing Riverview to sell to a favored developer. Why Riverview?

The answer to why Riverview closed is not an easy one. While racial tensions at the park were certainly higher than they had been in the past, as they were all over the United States, race did not play a significant factor in the closing. In his July 17, 1989 Chicago Tribune column, Mike Royko related the story of how he was responsible for getting the Dip attraction at Riverview closed. This attraction, which through the years had been

called the Nigger Dip, the Darktown Tangos, the Chocolate Drops, the African Dip, and finally the Dip, was the old dunk tank game with a difference - all or nearly all of the employees were African-American. Inside the dunk cages, men would shout insults like, "Hey Buddy, that's not the same girl you were with yesterday!". They tried to goad the person into purchasing a few balls to throw at the target, which if hit would send the man into the tank of water.

Royko witnessed this one day in the early 1960's and the following day he wrote a column about how it was disgraceful and racist. Riverview responded by removing the game within a few days. Six men, who were fired by the park, then went to Royko's office to ask him why he had written that column. As Royko quoted one of the workers, "I was making good money for shoutin' insults at a bunch of honkies and gettin' a little wet, and most of them couldn't throw good enough to put in the water one out of every 25 throws."

After Royko explained the social and moral issues involved, the worker then asked about the moral issue of him getting fired. Was Royko going to get him another job? Royko couldn't find them other jobs, but in his column he admitted he was right in theory, but possibly he'd been a little stupid in reality.

Perhaps Mike Royko's column started the news media thinking that there was a racial problem at Riverview? Some newspaper articles published shortly after the park closed insinuated that race was problem, but during our research, the worst thing we could validate was a case of African-American line-jumpers intimidating other patrons in line. The former park employees insisted that race relations were never a problem at Riverview.

The main reason the park closed was an economic one. The land the park occupied was worth much more than the revenue the park generated. Land that had been the outskirts of the city ninety years earlier, now was smack in the center. For two years prior to the closing of Riverview, the park stockholders received offers to sell their land.

When offers occurred, the Schmidt family convinced the other shareholders that the park was worth more to them intact. But as the value of the land grew, the offers became more frequent. The park was making money, but revenue was getting smaller, due to increasing labor, maintenance, and insurance costs. William B. Schmidt, George Schmidt's son and manager of the park, stated in October of 1967, "The attendance was down and costs were up. Last summer I had to pay $11 an hour for maintenance workers. You didn't have to pay a fraction of that in the '30's. It just became

harder and harder to make it pay". Keeping the stockholders happy became more and more difficult.

When George Schmidt died in 1957, he allegedly willed his stock to the United Charities of Chicago, which supposedly placed it in trust with a major local bank. Another of Riverview's major stockholders, Henry J. Merle, died in 1967. Henry Merle's stock was the same stock that William Merle originally purchased in April, 1912, from William M. Johnson, when Johnson was forced out of the company. According to former Riverview Purchasing Agent Chuck Simzyk, "In 1967 Henry J. Merle died and left 17 heirs. They wanted their money and forced the sale of the park." Mr. Merle's family allegedly decided to sell his stock to the same bank that already held the United Charities trust. The bank then became Riverview's primary stockholder and began approaching developers and informing them that "Riverview's property was for sale." The property was reportedly sold for approximately six

A Vaudeville show and the Chocolate Drops dunk tanks, just south of the main gate, circa 1915.

Close-up View of dunk tank.

The Darktown Tangos dunk tanks, circa 1921.

Laugh Your Troubles Away

Dunk tanks next to the coaster, early 1930's.

million dollars to a real estate man ironically named Edgar F. Grimm.

William B. Schmidt, tried desperately to stop the sale at the last stockholders meeting, but the stockholders voted to sell the property and dissolve the Riverview Park Company. Mr. Schmidt remarked the following day, "I only own less than 15 percent of the stock. When the trustees said, 'Look, this is it.', what could I do?". Why Mr. Schmidt did not try to finance a buyout of the other stockholders is unknown. For years after the park's closing, Mr. Schmidt refused to talk to people about the closing. Having the park taken away from him by bankers was just too painful to recall. As Schmidt told a reporter in 1967 who asked if he had a favorite ride, "OK, I don't want to get into that. It's just too sad. I can walk through the park and there's hardly an attraction I didn't work on or help build." The authors tried to

contact Mr. Schmidt while researching this book, but sadly, he passed away on June 21, 1993, about six months before we located his whereabouts in Florida. Riverview Park's former insurance agent settled his estate, as Schmidt apparently had no survivors.

The rides were sold at public auction on Friday, December 1, 1967. The park anticipated that their signature coaster, the world-famous Bobs, would bring a sale price of one million dollars. In fact, it brought no bids at all. Even when all of Riverview's coasters were offered as a package with the bids starting at $100,000, nobody wanted them! Traditional amusement parks were having a rough time during the 1960's, and as a result, no park was willing to pay even a couple of hundred thousand dollars to purchase a coaster that they would then have to dismantle, ship, and reassemble at their site. The smaller portable rides sold and

148

were scattered throughout the land.

Prior to the auction, the Philadelphia Toboggan Company was contacted to see if they were interested in purchasing Riverview's famous carousel or anything else from the park. John Allen sent back a bid of $2500 for the carousel's motor, power reducer, v-belt pulleys, an antelope carousel figure, and the control box for the Jetstream roller coaster. Realizing the carousel was worth far more, the bid was rejected by Edgar Grimm. According to one newspaper report, Chicago's Mayor Daley insisted the ride stay in Chicago, but the city never put in a bid. The Mayor's aide, Jack Reilly was quoted as saying after the auction, "Anyone who would pay that much for that thing is nuts."

The carousel was ultimately purchased by the City of Galena, Illinois, thanks to the timely intervention of Miss Jo Mead, who attended the auction preview. During the preview, Mead hurried to a phone and persuaded Galena's mayor, Robert Buehler to allow her to bid in the town's name. Miss Mead was authorized to bid up to $25,000 for the carousel, but she entered a first bid of only $15,000. That bid was not high enough, as the total for the carousel horses and frame sold piece by piece was higher. Galena later upped the bid to $25,000, but a $35,000 bid from Philadelphia forced the Mayor to up his bid to $40,000, which apparently would come from Mayor Buehler's own pocket. The owner of the Temple Steel company, Temple Smith, then placed a bid of $45,000, but somehow failed to get the payment in time to Edgar Grimm. Grimm needed to clear the park quickly, so he struck a deal with Buehler. Buehler would get the ride for $40,000 plus the $10,000 he would pay for shipping the ride to Galena.

As the carousel was packed for shipment from Chicago to Galena, three of the 72 horses disappeared. Two of the horses were the huge outside row standing figures, and one was a small inside one. The workers who dismantled the carousel were questioned, but the horses were never found. Mayor Buehler purchased the carousel with the hope of building a riverfront recreational center similar to Tivoli Gardens in Copenhagen, but he was unable to stir up enthusiasm for the project with the citizens of Galena. Frustrated and discouraged, Buehler sold the magnificent carousel in September, 1971, to the Six Flags Over Georgia Amusement Park for $53,000.

After the brokerage fees were paid, Buehler said he would just about get the $50,000 he'd already spent back. Six Flags eventually spent another $303,000 transporting, restoring, and building a new shelter for it. The new carousel building, which was designed before Six Flags knew the Riverview carousel was for sale, looks remarkably similar to Riverview's because the architect used his favorite carousel as a model - the one at Riverview Park, Chicago!

Also at the auction, the Jetstream coaster trains and hardware were sold to Sherwood Park, in Rockford, Illinois. Adventureland, in Addison, Illinois purchased the Fireball, Bobs, and Flash trains, along with two Shoot-the-Chutes boats, the Boomerang cars, and the Strat-O-Stat cars. Also sold to Adventureland was the Aladdin's Castle facade for around $9000. Adventureland moved the coaster trains from Riverview on a flatbed semi-truck. Upon leaving the park, train one of the Flash was wrecked when it was driven into a viaduct without sufficient clearance.

Laugh Your Troubles Away

Canille Perille paints the Carousel horses.

In 1969, the owner of Adventureland died and the trains were sold for $500. The trains were stored in Momence, Illinois, and later moved to the Wisconsin Dells. The Fireball and Flash trains were moved back to Momence in 1971, while the Bobs trains were moved there in May 1980. The Fireball trains were sold to the Carowinds Theme Park in the Carolinas for $6300. Carowinds wanted to purchase the Flash trains, but the owner refused because he was emotionally attached to them. Carowinds ran the Fireball and Jetstream trains on the Thunder Road coaster, but was forced to remove them when the unusually heavy trains caused the coaster structure to deteriorate at an unacceptable rate. The Bubble Bounce ride and half of the Hot Rod cars ended up at an amusement park in Salt Lake City. The Ferris Wheel and the Paratrooper rides went to Playland, on the

south side of Chicago. The Whip ended up in Ohio, and the Bump 'Em and Wild Mouse rides were removed by the concessionaires that owned them. The Caterpillar and Tilt-A-Whirl rides were bulldozed after they were not removed. The Aladdin's Castle facade was acquired by Ralph Lopez from Adventureland. He later sold it to Bally's Aladdin's Castle Arcade in the early 1980's. Its whereabouts are currently unknown.

Mr. Grimm began receiving death threats for his part in closing Riverview and expressed amazement over the publicity to the Chicago papers. Grimm decided to hold a meeting on October 5th, 1967, to see if the park could be reopened for a one-day whoop-de-do farewell party. The idea was abandoned because of the uncertain fall weather and the problem of getting trained people to operate the rides. Most of Riverview's staff had gone on to other jobs. Mr. Grimm ended up tripling the number of night guards at the park from six to eighteen to deter souvenir seekers. Said a Grimm spokesperson, "Some kids are even getting on skiffs, floating down the river and trying to get in. We've also had a number of calls from crackpots threatening us for closing down Riverview."

Also discussed at the same meeting was the job futures of the forty or so year round employees. "They offered us jobs at Transo Envelope Company", says Ralph Lopez. Rumors floated around that the City of Chicago would purchase the park's rides and move them to a city park, but this just turned out to be wishful thinking.

Within a week of the property's sale, the Arvey Corporation purchased the land from Mr. Grimm and began clearing it for redevelopment. Many people took photographs and films as the park was being torn down. It was heart-wrenching to watch a Comet train being used as a wrecking ball to demolish the rest of the coaster structure.

The original development plans for the Riverview site called for a United Parcel Service industrial building right on Western Avenue. After much discussion, UPS was convinced to move their planned building to the back of the acreage, allowing a shopping mall to be built at the front. Soon, the first buildings including the State Farm Insurance building and a Chicago Police headquarters began to appear on the site. UPS eventually decided to build their depot elsewhere, so their acreage was sold to provide land for the DeVry Institute of Technology.

The Riverview Roller Rink continued to operate while the developers tried to find a buyer for the land it occupied. The rink organist, Russ Young, and his partner, Arthur Buckwinkler, leased the rink from the new owners. It remained a popular hangout until a spectacular fire on the night of June 16, 1971, burned it to the ground. As the fire broke out at 6:45pm, many in the neighborhood ran over to the rink, fearing that kids were inside. Luckily, skating was scheduled only on Thursday, Saturday, and Sunday nights, so no one was in the building at the time of the blaze.

All that is left of Riverview today is a small city park on the east bank of the Chicago River. It survived because the river was widened, deepened, and straightened by the City of Chicago Sanitary District between 1904 and 1909, and they had title to a 90 foot channel and a 40 foot bank on either side of the river between Belmont and Lawrence streets. The section of river behind the park was worked on in 1909. Rather than face a long court battle over that strip of land, the developer decided to work with the city to provide a park there. Today, one can see the concrete remains of the Midway, the Carousel Building, the Shoot-The-Chutes, and even the Comet. If you are ever in Atlanta, stop at Six Flags Over Georgia amusement park and visit the only remaining ride from Riverview - the magnificent Carousel. It is well maintained and available for a ride into the past.

Numerous attempts have been made over the last 32 years to rebuild Riverview at a different location. In 1968, Howard Ryerson opened a new Riverview Park in Bruce, Wisconsin. The park contained the former Riverview's Hot Rods, Crazy Dazy, and train rides, along with a Ferris Wheel, Carousel, Kiddy rocket ship and roller coaster rides that were purchased elsewhere. The park closed after the 1970 season. Mrs. Ryerson commented to co-author Ralph Lopez that they discovered that people came to Bruce, Wisconsin for hunting and fishing, not for amusement rides.

Riverview has not been forgotten by the citizens of Chicago and references to it are everywhere. On June 1, 1980, artwork by local artist Jerry Peart, entitled "Riverview", was erected in front of the police headquarters on the former Riverview site. The sculpture's colors, blue, red, white, and yellow, are supposed to represent a different part of Riverview. A play was written in 1992 that used Riverview as its setting. Titled Riverview: A Melodrama with Music, it was written by John Logan and opened June 22nd at the Goodman Theatre in Chicago. Those persons who had visited the real Riverview disliked the production because as one person described it, "It made the place seem tawdry." The play used themes of sharp, violent conflict, and included dialogue that was typical of gangsters and molls. In the view of these audiences, the play did not reflect what Riverview was about at all. Riverview was a happy place right to the park's closing.

Riverview has left a legacy of cherished memories and fascinating photographs. In the end, Riverview Park lived up to the Creed that it published in 1933:

"To provide clean safe, wholesome outdoor recreation for everybody;

To fill the hearts of children with joy while spending their hours of play in the sunshine and fresh air.

To treat our patrons as our guests and by our courteous manner make them our friends who will look upon our park with pride and as a benefit to the community;

To send every man, woman and child home feeling that the time has been well spent and eager to return."

Showboat

Riverview Park Attractions

1896 - 1903

Carousel (E. Joy Morris built)
Ferris Wheel
Games Booths

1904

The White Flyer (Figure-8 coaster)
Shooting the Rapids
The Temple of Mirth
A Trip to the Mines
Helter Skelter
Hiawatha Village
Radium Palace

1906

Over the Waves
Rollin's Wild Animal Arena
Dancing Pavilion (later used as a Roller Rink in the 1940's)
Igorrote Indian Village
Ostrich Farm
Crocodile Ranch
Hale's Tours of the World
Double Whirl
Aero-Stat
The Fall of Pompeii fireworks
Casino restaurant

1907

The Pike (midway) constructed
Front Gate
Lagoon
Velvet Coaster
Hellgate
The Top
Pikes Peak Scenic Railway
Fairyland section built
Shoot-The-Chutes
Marine Causeway built
Baseball diamond
Roller Skating in picnic grounds
Aquarasel

1908

Royal Gorge Scenic Railway
Aerial Coaster (renamed Pottsdam Railway in 1909)
Monitor and Merrimac
Thousand Islands
Carousel (Philadelphia Toboggan Company #17)
Eye-Full Tower
The Fight of the Little Big Horn
Whirlpool

1909

Creation
Tickler
Witching Waves
Expo Whirl
Buffalo Bill's Wild West and Pawnee Bill's Far East combined show
Duncan Clark's Hook Bazar (amateur contest)
Seven Temptations of Good Old St. Anthony (motion picture)

1910

The Derby
Atlantic Beach

1911

Blue Streak
Motordrome
Autodrome

1912

Dante's Inferno (motion picture)
Gee Whiz (aka Greyhound)
"Daredevil" Schreyer

1913

Sinking of the Titanic
Arthur Pryor's Band
Gyroplane
Palais Pictorial
Mardi Gras Parade Begins

1914

Jack Rabbit
War of the Worlds

1915

Velodrome
Waterdrome
Panama Canal Show

1916

Battles of a Nation
Ostrich and Alligator Farm
Sea Cows (Manatees)
Snoozer, the talking Dog

Riverview Park Attractions

1917

Bug House
Whip

1918

Over the Falls

1919

Ginger Snap (aka Virginia Reel or Crazy Ribbon)
The Winner
Cannon Ball
League of Notions Show

1920

Ferris Wheel
Hey Day
Skedaddle
Big Dipper (aka the Zephyr and the Comet)
Noah's Ark
Stop! Look! Loosen! Show

1921

The Pippin (aka the Silver Flash or the Flash)
Dodge-Em's
Aerojoy Plane
Puzzle Town
Pony ride
Mill on the Floss
Smiles of 1921 Show
Fort Dearborn Massacre (Firework show)
Great Chicago Fire (Firework show)
Le Grand Fete da Fea (Festival of Fire) - Firework
show

1922

Evans and Gordan Famous Collection of Freak
Animals

1923

Skyrocket (aka Blue Streak, Fireball)
Caterpillar
Dr. Browning's Curiosities
Greyhound Racing

1924

Bobs

1925

Santa Fe Miniature Railway
Wax museum
Man-ape

1926

Kiddy Land
Kiddy Bobs
Free Circus

1927

Bicycle Rental
Electric Fountain

1928

Tilt-A-Whirl

1929 -1930

No new attractions known

1931

Spook Town

1932

Aladdin's Castle

1933

Hell 'n' Back Funhouse (aka Hades)
A Century of Nonsense Show

1934

Two Cent Days and Five Cent Nights Admission

1935

Flying Turns
Motordrome (moved from World's Fair)
Flying Scooters
Two Big Eli No. 16 Ferris Wheels

1936

Pair-O-Chutes
Midget Auto Racing (professional racers)
Indianapolis Race Track (ride)

1937

Cuddle-Up
Strat-O-Stat

1938

Octopus

Riverview Park Attractions

1939

Boomerang

1940

Sky Ride (a Sky Wheel Ferris Wheel)
Streamline Pacific miniature train
Moon Rocket
Roll-O-Plane
Magic Trees Lighting in Hippodrome section

1941-1942

No new attractions known

1943

Dive Bomber

1944-1945

No new attractions known

1946

Bubble Bounce

1947

No new attractions known

1948

Riverview Scout & Chief miniature trains
Water Bug

1949-1950

No new attractions known

1951

Kiddy Tumble Bug
Tunnel of Love

1952

Rotor

1953

You and the Atom

1954

Hot Rods
Flying Cars

1955

No new attractions known

1956

Ghost Train
Jet Rocket

1957

Showboat

1958

Wild Mouse

1959

Fireball
Moving Eyes on Aladdin's Castle
Date Night Hops

1960

Paratrooper
Safari dark ride
Kiddy Helicopter

1961

Kiddy Carousel
Calypso
Mountain Road (Matterhorn)

1962

Crazy Dazy

1963

Space Ride (Von-Roll Sky Ride)

1964

The Twist (aka Trabant)

1965

Jetstream

1966

Bump'em (renovated Dodge-ems)

THE COASTERS OF RIVERVIEW

Name of Operation	Seasons	Designer/Builder
White Flyer (Figure-8)	1904 - early '20s	L.A. Thompson Co.
Pikes Peak Scenic Railway	1907 - 1911 Removed for Gee Whiz	Miller/Thompson/Barry
The Top	1907 - 1916	Spiral Wheel Operating Corporation
Royal Gorge Scenic Railway	1908 - 1920 Torn down for Pippin	Miller/Barry
Aerial Coaster (a.k.a. Pottsdam Railway)	1908 - 1910 Removed for Blue Streak	Aerial Tramway Construction Company
Velvet Coaster	1909 - 1919 Removed for Big Dipper	Federal Construction Co.
Derby (Racing Coaster)	1910 - 1931 Burned in Apr. 1932 Bug House fire	Miller/Ingersoll
Blue Streak #1	1911 - 1923 Removed for Bobs	Miller/Ingersoll
Gee Whiz (a.k.a. Greyhound)	1912 - 1963 Removed for Jetstream	Miller
Jack Rabbit	1914 - 1932 Used for maintenance lumber.	Miller/Ingersoll
The Cannon Ball	1919 -1925 Proposed for Royal Gorge site but was not built there. Was built on Western Ave. Parking lot site. Lost its lease.	Miller, Benjamin E. Winslow Built by F. W. Pearce

THE COASTERS OF RIVERVIEW

Name of Operation	Seasons	Designer/Builder
Big Dipper a.k.a. Zephyr a.k.a. Comet	1920 - 1967 1936 - 1939 1940 - 1967 Had 17 dips. Went from 4 Car trains to 5 car trains in 1966. Also got new platform and transfer table that year.	Miller/Baker
The Pippin a.k.a. Silver Flash a.k.a. Flash	1921 - 1937 1938 - 1960 1961 - 1967	Miller/Baker designed 10/16/20
Skyrocket a.k.a. Blue Streak #2 a.k.a. Fireball	1923 - 1935 1936 - 1958 1959 - 1967	Miller/Baker designed 11/20/22 for Belmont Construction Co. Plans Plans revised by park to straighten turnaround.
The Bobs	1924 - 1967	Prior & Church design. Construction by Gierke & Traver
Kiddie Bobs	1926 - 1934	Prior & Church
Flying Turns	1935 - 1967	Miller & Bartlett Purchased used from World's Fair.
Wild Mouse	1958 - 1967	Ben Schiff
Jetstream	1964 - 1967	John Allen/PTC cost $303,756.77 to build.

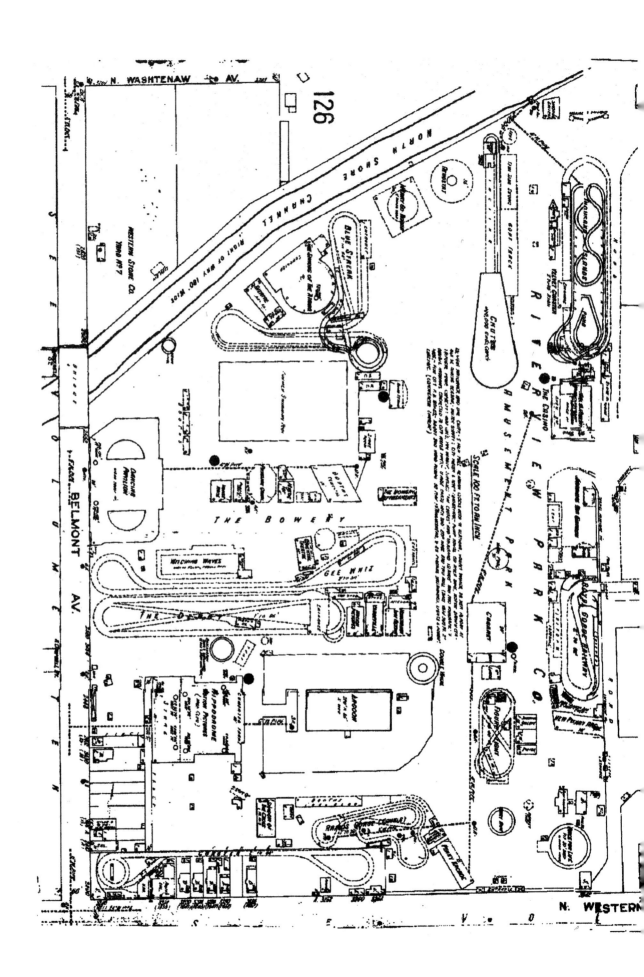

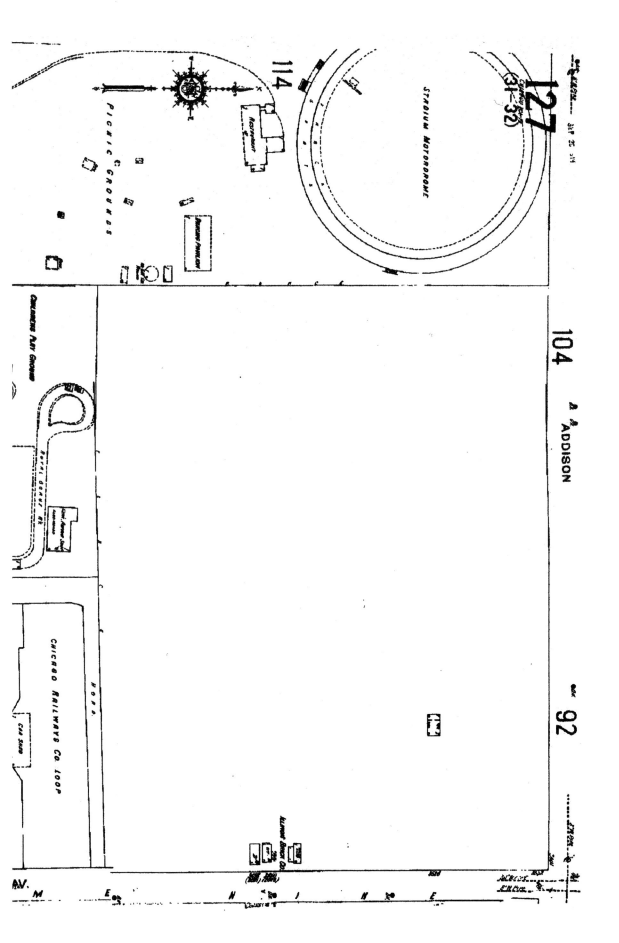

Riverview park - 1913

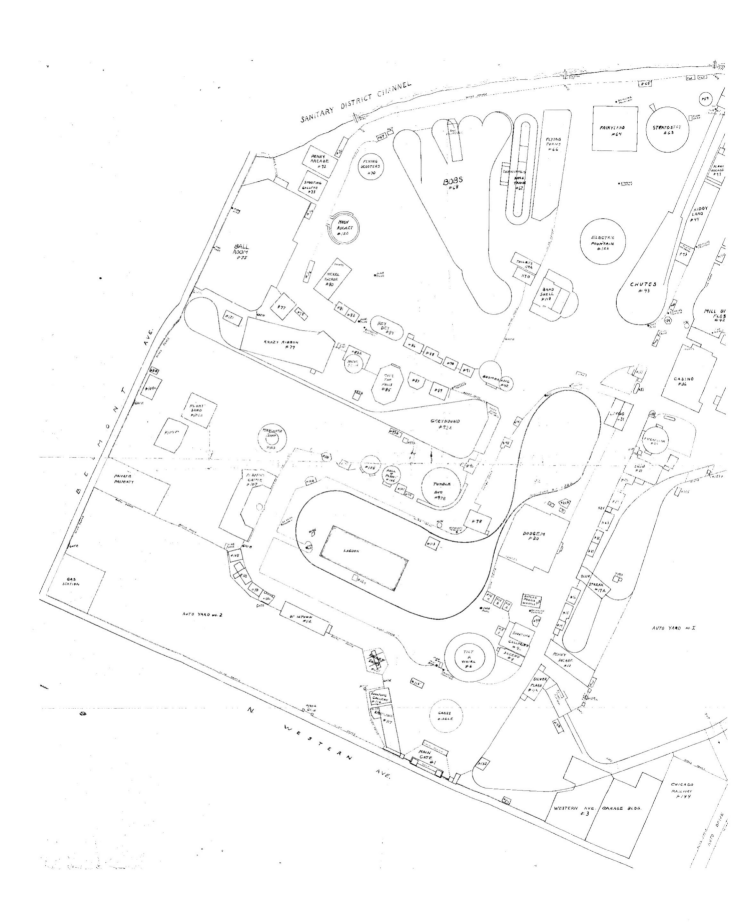

Topographical Map - Riverview park - 1939

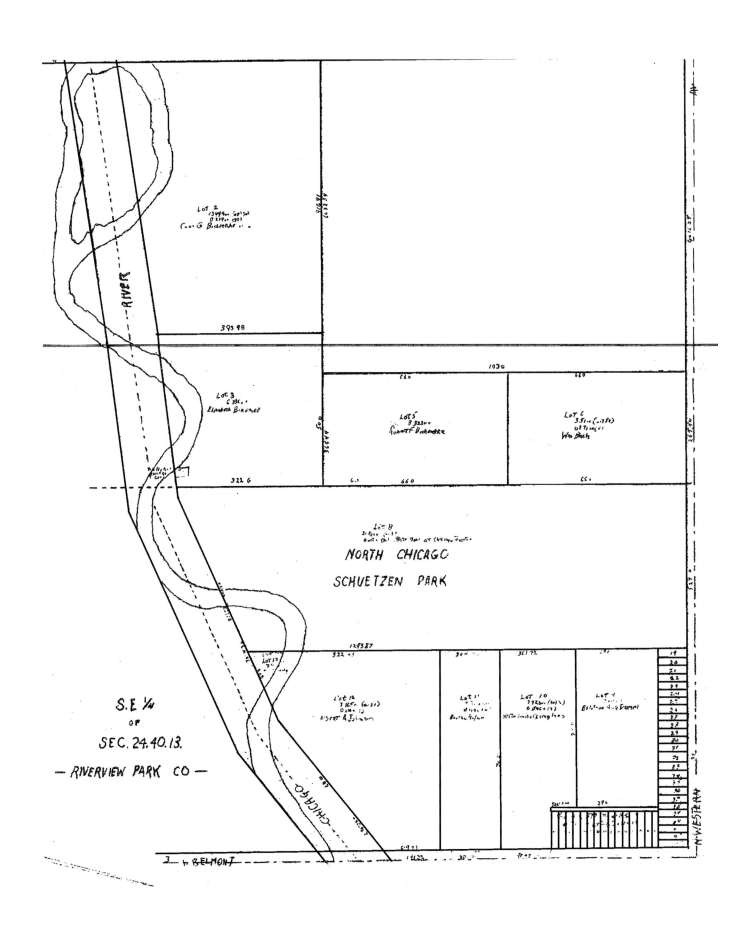

Riverview park - 1907 map showing river being straightened

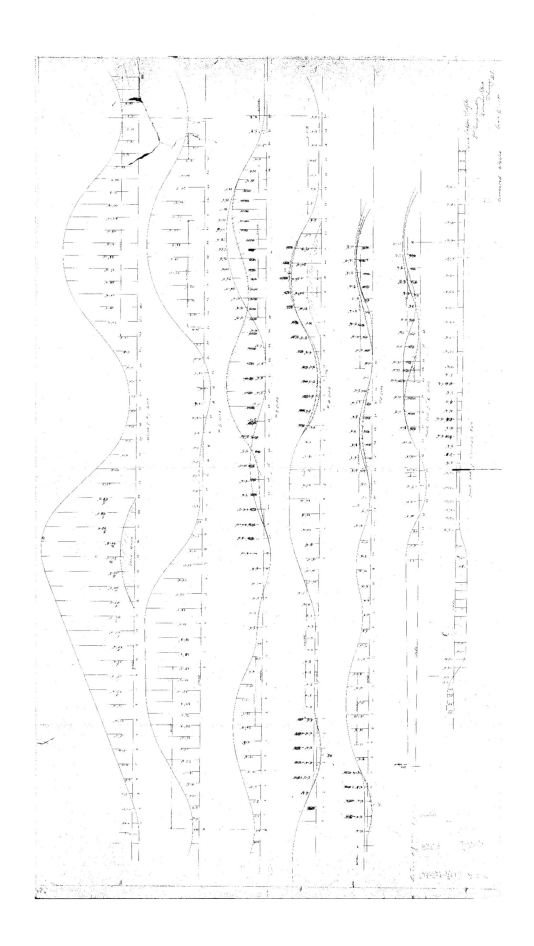

The Bob's Profile

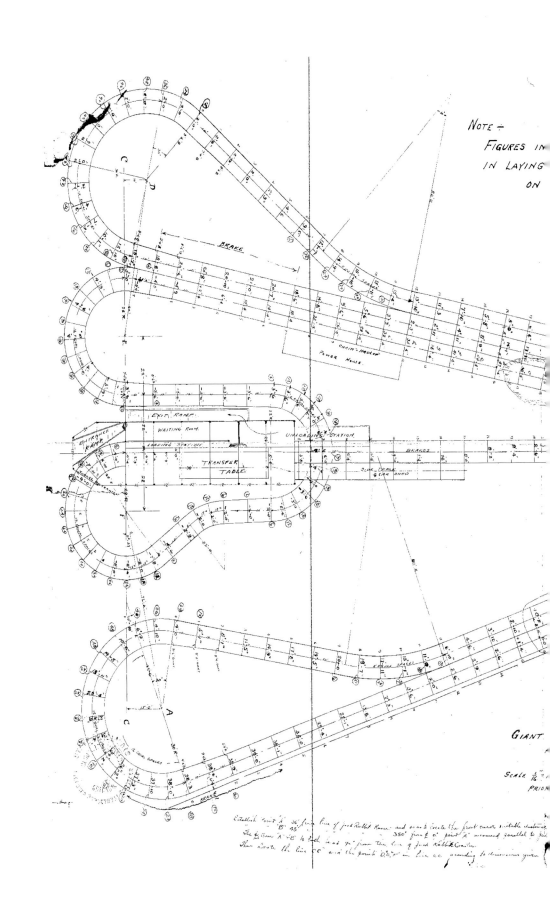

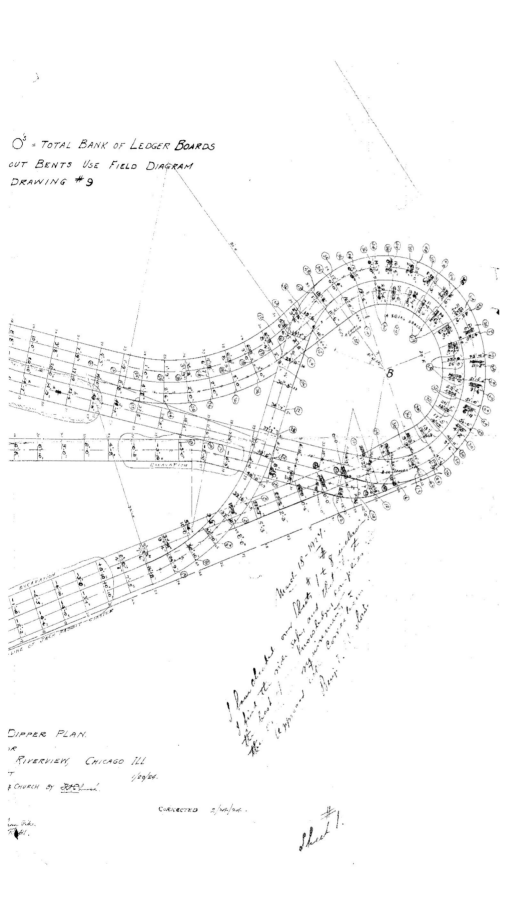

The Bob's Coaster

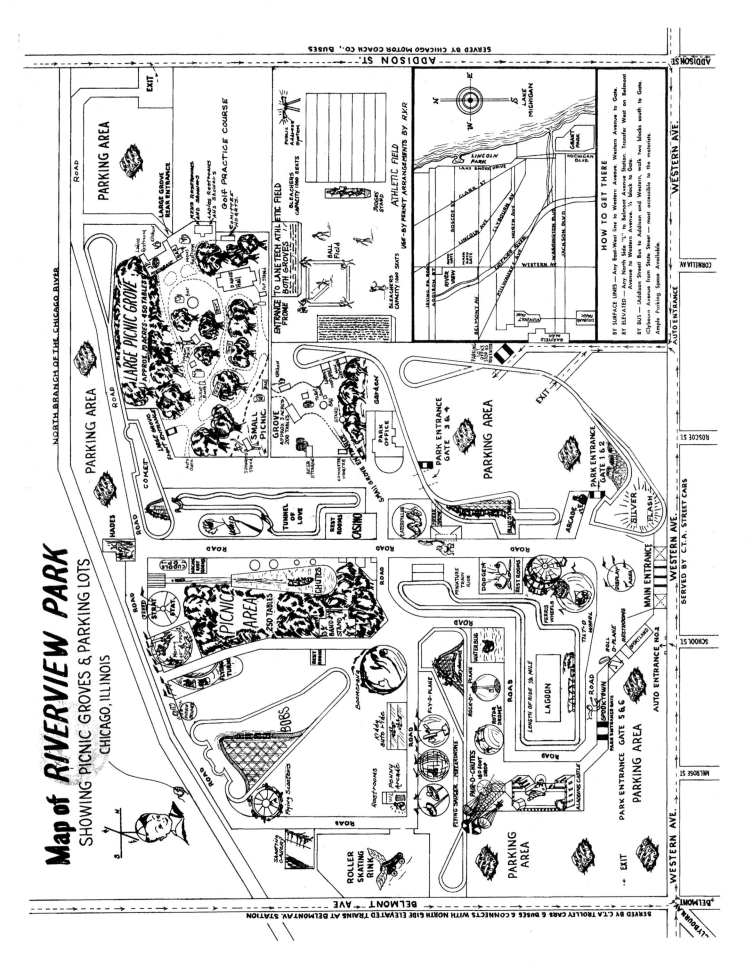

Map of *RIVERVIEW PARK*
SHOWING PICNIC GROVES & PARKING LOTS
CHICAGO, ILLINOIS

Riverview park - Early 1950's